Miles to Go:

A Lifetime of Running and Bicycling Adventures

DAVID LYGRE

ISBN: 1497394201
ISBN-13: 978-1497394209

DEDICATION

To my wife, Laurae, and our children, Lindsay and Jedd. Thanks for letting me go outside and play.

TABLE OF CONTENTS

DAVID LYGRE

1 LAST MILES, ALMOST

The plan was simple. My wife, Laurae, and I would drive my sisters to Yakima for their early flight out, grab a bite of breakfast, and then she'd drop me off north of Selah. I'd run the 25 miles back to Ellensburg on a remote jeep road while she drove home on the freeway in time to go to church.

It was early December, 2007 in Washington state. The road was snowy and the forecast called for one inch of new snow and a southerly (tail) wind. Just to be on the safe side, I carried an extra shirt, rain poncho, wool socks and running pants in my back pack. I'd run this route dozens of times, often in winter, though rarely alone and never in this direction. I looked forward to the adventure.

As dawn broke I said good-bye to Laurae and ran a couple miles on a paved road before turning onto the dirt and graveled Sheep Company Road that angled north to Ellensburg. The snowy blanket crunched under each step in the silent, windless morning. At intersecting roads I hadn't noticed running from the other direction, I turned around and looked back, knowing what the landscape looked like facing south. The route was easy to find and I felt strong. A few hunters drove by, their vehicles leaving a nice tread in the snow.

In my running pants, long-sleeve shirt topped with a tank top, stocking cap and gloves I was warm, almost too warm. Eight miles passed pleasantly before I noticed a gentle snow and tail wind. At this rate I would get home two hours before the 4 p.m. I had estimated for Laurae. As the snow deepened, the vehicle tracks still made a perfect surface for running. *You fools, thank you,* I thought. Then I met the "fools" driving back.

The climb up the south flank of North Umtanum Ridge began. I hiked the winding road as the snow thickened and the wind strengthened. I recognized the sharp switchback and knew I'd soon be on top and into the home half of the run: three more miles down to Umtanum Creek, four miles up to the end of Durr Road, and then six paved miles home.

Before noon, near the top of the ridge, the wind howled and snow thickened, making it hard to see. *Where's the road? It must be the white lane between the sagebrush and rocks. There's a green-dot sign to mark the road. I'm getting cold. Where does the road go from here? I'll try this way. I don't recognize this next post, so I better go back to the green-dot sign and try again. I'm back at the sign, but now where do I go?*

I was getting very cold. The wind near the top of the ridge

was screaming, pushing me up into snow knee-deep in places and into a nearly total whiteout. *What should I do?* I thought about getting more calories into my body, but all my fuel was inside water bottles, and I couldn't stand the thought of drinking ice-cold liquid.

I dimly saw some kind of structure along a string of fence posts. *Oh, it's just a pile of rocks, but maybe it will give me some shelter.* I lay beside it with my rain poncho at the best angle to shield the wind. The poncho flapped ferociously. *This shelter just isn't good enough. I have to do something else.*

Should I turn around and go back to Selah? I can't see my tracks or the road back, and I'd be going into the teeth of the wind. And it's seven or eight miles in either direction to the nearest house. Going back won't work.

My legs were post-holing in the snow, so I tried to find a drift where I could dig a hole for shelter. *I've heard of people doing that.* I found some deep, sticky snow. It was hard to scoop out enough to make a hole for my whole body, so I pushed with my feet to enlarge the hole just enough to crawl in. I lay motionless on my side, scarcely able to move, bent into a fetal position, as new snow began to cover me. The hole gave shelter from the wind, but my clothes were wet and I was cold even though I'd put on everything in my pack.

Is this the right thing to do? If I could just get over the top of this ridge and find the road going down I'd have less wind to deal with and could probably make it to Ellensburg. But I can't see ahead, my sense of direction is poor, I'm not sure exactly where I am, and if I go over the ridge in the wrong direction I'll be in territory where Search and Rescue would never find me. Yet to stay here, as cold as I am, is risky, too. I don't know how long I can last like this.

I had to try. I crawled out of my hole, held my poncho tightly as the wind whipped at it, and tried to figure out where to go. I couldn't. I had a sense of what was uphill, but no sense of direction and couldn't see anything. *It would be crazy to just charge uphill and hope for the best.* Reluctantly, I crammed myself back into the snow hole. Making a run for it, whatever the logic, was not an option. I'd have to survive in this snow hole if I was going to make it.

Hours passed. *Did I hear something? Listen again, carefully. Just the wind, I guess. If no one finds me I'll stay here until 7 a.m. That will give enough time, I hope, for the storm to pass, dawn will be breaking, and maybe Search and Rescue will out be looking for me. I need to be out for them to find me.*

I could barely move inside my snow hole. I was shivering and my muscles were cramping. I tried to get through the next fifteen minutes, and then the next fifteen. My stocking cap and wool socks, and another pair of wool socks for mittens worked well, but my torso was very cold. I'd lost some feeling in my toes hours ago. Maybe frostbite.

I really might not make it. My retirement, scheduled for next June, might come a few months early. Who will give my students their final exams and grade them? At least I made up the exams, and my colleagues will find them on the desk in my office.

What will people think if I die? It will be hard on Laurae and our children. At least they have the skills and resources to get on with their lives. Some people will say: "He died doing what he loves to do." My sisters and Laurae (and the other members of her music trio) will feel guilty about their schedule causing me to run alone today instead of on Saturday with my running friends. They shouldn't feel that way, but they will.

I hear hypothermia isn't a bad way to die. You just gradually lose consciousness and then it's over. Why can't I just go to sleep? It's all that shivering and cramping. Isn't the human body marvelous the way shivering generates heat when you need it?

What's wrong with you? Why are you thinking about dying when your brain is working fine? Use it to figure out how to survive.

Eighteen cold hours passed incredibly slowly, but they passed. The worst moment came when I looked at my watch, with its faintly lit face, and realized I had misread the time earlier and had six hours longer to wait than I had thought.

Finally it was almost 7 a.m., time to crawl out and face my fate. *If I can't figure out where I am now, I probably won't make it.*

I was wedged so tightly in the hole I couldn't get much leverage to dig out. A sky light into the hole showed where to dig. After fifteen minutes of slight motions and moving small bits of snow, I took a deep breath and left my snowy tomb. The next thirty seconds would reveal whether I was more likely to live or die today.

The wind and snow had stopped; the storm had passed. In the early morning light I saw, fifty yards away, what looked like a very tall hitching post. *Could that possibly be what I'd been trying to find before I crawled into the snow hole, the structure at the top of North Umtanum Ridge on Durr Road?*

I had to get a closer look, but my muscles were so spent that I couldn't stand. I crawled in the snow along the fence line toward the post. It was indeed the landmark I desperately hoped it was. I was eight miles from where anyone lived, and thirteen miles from home, but I knew where I was. *Somehow, I will get to Ellensburg.*

After several attempts, I struggled to my feet. I couldn't lift or straighten my head; my neck was too sore from being bent all night. My back pack was lost near the snow hole, and it was twenty hours since I'd had anything to eat or drink, but I didn't need it. I knew I'd dehydrate more slowly in this cold weather, and I had enough body fat to fuel me home.

I saw snowmobile tracks on the road. *Did Search and Rescue come by earlier? Did I miss them? Was that the sound I thought I heard last night while I was in my snow hole?* I walked unsteadily down the jeep road, through thick slush and streams of ice water. The temperature was above freezing, but I was wet and chilled to the bone. Feeling gradually returned to my feet. After three miles I reached Umtanum Creek and walked straight through. With feet already ice-cold and soaked, there was no point trying to cross carefully. Up the next hill, a four-mile climb, again in slush and streaming ice water.

While I pondered my predicament, I realized a deep, primordial instinct, bent only on survival, was taking over my body. *Keep walking. It's all you can do. No more decisions to make. No more options. Keep walking until you get help.*

A mile from the end of Durr Road, two miles from the nearest house and seven miles from home, a vehicle approached. *I have to get a ride, no matter what.* I raised my arms for them to stop and recognized the driver, Brett Wenger, who was with another Search and Rescue volunteer, Bill Hunt. They said they were looking for me.

"Get in," they said. I couldn't; my leg muscles just wouldn't climb into their SUV. They helped me in and turned up the heater.

"Take off your wet clothes," they said. I couldn't; those muscles didn't work, either. They put dry clothes on me and handed me a cup of warm tea. I was shivering and shaking, more depleted than I had realized. They radioed in that they'd found me and drove a mile to a road where they handed me off to an EMT.

The EMT asked me to get into the ambulance. I couldn't, so he put me on a stretcher, hoisted me in, and checked my vital signs. He pulled a thermometer out of my mouth and said, "Ninety-two degrees." I could only wonder how low it had been four hours earlier. The EMT wanted me to check in at the hospital, but I signed papers so I could just go home.

I hobbled into my home and was welcomed by about thirty people, including two doctors, two nurses (including Laurae) and our daughter, Lindsay. I was overwhelmed by all the kind, caring, worried people who had been searching and praying for me since yesterday. As he watched Dr. Wickerath administer the first of two bags of warm saline solution through the needle in my arm, the EMT agreed I was getting excellent care here.

"Can you talk to reporters from TV stations driving up from Yakima?"

"Okay."

"How about newspaper reporters from Ellensburg and

Yakima?"

"Okay."

They arrived, we talked, and as they left they give us a news update: two people had died in the storm so far and several others were still missing.

Christmas came early this year. I'm going to live.

2 FIRST MILES

Scientists haven't discovered a gene for rambling, so my itchy feet might have come from my father, a Lutheran minister and missionary, or from his father, a Glendive, Montana railroad man who was often out on the rails. Dad believed that after five years it was best for both the pastor and congregation to move on, so we did. He also took long summer vacation trips, packing his family of six and one large tent into our car and driving to every corner of the country, stopping at every monument and national park along the way. By the time I'd finished high school, I had set foot in almost all of the states and lived in five Midwestern states, plus South Africa and Argentina.

Mom liked to travel, too. She was the daughter of a missionary to what was then Persia, who translated the Bible into the Kurdish language, and who died mysteriously, probably poisoned by a local who didn't appreciate his missionary zeal. She grew up wanting to be a missionary's wife and eagerly accompanied Dad to South Africa in the 1940s to work with Zulu people.

Whenever Dad received a "call" to go to a new church, he would take about two weeks to discern God's will before deciding. During that, for me, mysterious process, I always prayed the Lord would reveal to Dad that he should accept the call so I could see what the new place looked like.

So after six years in Ellensburg, Washington, the longest I'd lived anywhere, my feet were itching again. But I also knew I had a great situation. In the mid-1970s I was busy raising a family and teaching biochemistry at what is now Central Washington University. Laurae was taking time out from her school nurse job to have more time with our young son, Jedd. Soon our daughter, Lindsay, would grace our family.

I loved teaching and felt lucky to be in such a good school and location. The university had about 7000 students, which matched the population of the rest of our town, an interesting mix of university folks, business people, and ranchers. Nestled along the Yakima River in a broad valley on the dry side of the state, Ellensburg had four-season weather and mountains in three directions that beckoned to us to play outside every chance we got.

To slake my wanderlust, I would take my family on sabbatical leaves every chance I got in the next two decades, spending the better part of a year each in England, New Zealand, and Australia.

Each time we would return to Ellensburg, refreshed and ready to keep living there.

But early in my Ellensburg years, a cloud was looming. I remember the exact moment it hit me. On opening day of city league softball season a fly ball was screaming toward me in left field. I raced after it and dove for the ball, trying to keep my eye on it while making a back-handed catch. The ball hit my glove and bounced away. It wasn't an easy catch, but it was one I knew I should have made.

What's wrong? Maybe my eye-hand coordination is slipping a bit. Then I also noticed that love handles were creeping out on my body, and my weight was creeping upward. It dawned on me: *when you're age 34, you don't get fitness for free any more.*

I grumbled within earshot of a Chemistry Department friend, Clint Duncan. A few years older than me, he'd been there. He nodded and told me his secret: at noon each day he slipped over to the campus gym to jog or use exercise machines. He mentioned that a few supermen and women there ran a four-mile loop before returning to work. He wondered if I would like to try running.

My mind drifted back to 9th grade, in Yankton, South Dakota, the only time I had tried running. My claim to fame, later, was that one year ahead of me in school was Tom Brokaw, who you might have heard of.

One day my friend, Leland, said, "Let's go out for track."

I shrugged and said, "Okay."

We reported to the gym, got our gear and assigned lockers, and ran a few blocks to the track. We jogged around the track while Coach talked with the real athletes, those who played football for him. The stars did their own drills, depending on which events they were working on. The rest of us had no events; we just jogged until practice was over.

One day was different. That day Coach actually spoke to a few of us scrubs, telling us to line up and run 100 yards against his top sprinter (and halfback). To his surprise, and mine, I crossed the line even with his sprinter. In disbelief, Coach asked just the two of us to race again. This time his sprinter beat me by a step. His pecking order restored, Coach silently smiled and resumed working with his athletes.

Leland and I kept going to practice, jogging around and watching the team members doing their drills. Several weeks later he told me he thought there were actually track meets at which the regulars participated. But I doubted it; I hadn't seen or heard anything about them. After eight weeks Leland said he thought track season was over, so we stopped going. Later I learned the season was still going. It didn't matter.

That memory, and my reluctance to become a Pillsbury Doughboy, spurred me to tell Clint I would try running. Four miles was out of the question, of course, but maybe I could run one. I went to the gym with him, got a locker, and gasped four laps around the track. A few weeks later, one mile became two. In a few months, I was one of the people circling the four-mile loop at noon. Flab was disappearing.

Then Clint told me about a 10-km (6.2-mile) race in the Yakima Canyon that was open to anyone—even a novice like me. I gulped and decided to enter. The day before the race I bought my first pair of real running shoes, blue-and-white beauties, but felt both guilty at the price and unworthy to be wearing Adidas.

On race morning I drove through the canyon, paying close attention to the course I would soon be running, and parked near the finish line. There we runners were herded into National Guard trucks and driven to the start. We lined up behind a chalk line drawn across the road. The starting gun released 300 runners and all of my adrenalin.

Mile one was flat and easy. I felt strong as we raced along the Yakima River, drinking in the views. Much of mile two climbed a hill where I had planned to take a few walk breaks. But the juice was flowing and so was I. I flew up that hill and tore down the other side, reaching the three-mile mark and hearing a split time that was faster than I had ever run three miles. A small voice inside said, "Uh-oh." That voice also reminded me I'd never run more than four miles.

I kept charging but the pain was gaining. At four miles, where the course flattened and I had planned to make my move, my only move was to survive. My legs turned into wooden posts and the young girl down the street who babysat for us was gaining ground. I desperately tried to stay ahead.

The final mile held an endless curve that concealed the finish line. People passed as I moved in slow motion. Finally I saw Laurae and Jedd cheering as the finish line came into view, and I staggered across it. A couple minutes later I watched a slightly blue friend, gasping for breath, cross that line and immediately receive oxygen from the medical staff.

While I gathered my breath, I thought about some lessons I'd learned: *don't go out too fast; you need some longer training runs; and if you can't handle being beaten by women, you'll have to find a different sport.* Those lessons didn't really matter, though, because I promised I'd never race again.

Three days later I asked Clint if he knew of any more races. He did, but he had something else in mind for me. He was getting grumpy about me passing him when we ran at noon, so he planned his final move carefully.

He told me about the signature hike on the outskirts of Ellensburg, a trail that climbed nearly 2000 feet in two miles. One sunny, summer day he drove us out to Manashtash Ridge and told me a couple of things: the last part was the steepest; and he thought the course record was 24 minutes.

Now a veteran of one 10-km race, I took the bait. We jogged together along an irrigation canal until we reached a telephone pole, where the timing was to begin. He pointed out the trail to our left, we started our watches, and I charged up the first of four uphill sections, quickly leaving him in the dust. I slipped a few times on the steep grade, not being used to running on dirt, and increased the pace on the next, gentler uphill section. The trail up the third major hill wound through trees that provided welcome shade on the hot day.

But I was wilting. My lungs were burning and my legs were rubber as I bent over, bracing my hands on my knees to keep them from buckling. Just one more step. Then one more. Then one more. Finally, the trees gave way to the final, steepest section. The top was in clear sight, but it blurred as I collapsed.

Two thoughts went through my mind. First, *how will they land a helicopter on the side of this hill to get me out?* Second, I remembered watching a tape of the 1908 Olympic Games in London where the marathon leader, Italian Dorando Pietri, entered the stadium and collapsed, less than a lap from the finish line. Several times he got up, and each time he fell back down. As he lay on the track, several runners passed him and finished.

Finally he was helped to his feet and disqualified.

When I watched that tape I had said to myself: *there is no way a person can't finish that short, final distance if he is mentally strong enough.* But lying broken on Manashtash Ridge, closer to the top than Dorando Pietri was to his finish line, I realized I was wrong. *There are physical limits, no matter how tough you are.*

Ten minutes later, when Clint hiked by, I explained that I'd been to the summit and was waiting for him. But he'd have none of it. His grin was a mile wide as he hiked to the top and returned to me. Eventually a miracle occurred and I was able to hobble down the hill with him to his truck. There he checked the thermometer and announced it was 106 degrees. His grin widened.

3 ONE HUNDRED MILES

The late 1970s swept many of us into America's running boom. I devoured *The Complete Book of Running* by Jim Fixx and started learning how to train and what shoes to wear. I ruefully cheered "Amen" when I read his advice that when you are running and are attacked by a dog, don't expect the dog's owner to stick up for you.

My learning curve was steep. A few weeks after my first 10-km race, a new 10-km race sprang up in town. I calculated that to break forty minutes—my goal—I'd have to average just under 6:30 per mile. Knowing the course, I had carefully planned how fast to run each mile. On race day I reached one mile, feeling good until the race official called out my time: 5:45. *Oops. Way too fast.* I dialed it back and at two miles heard 14:30. *Oops again. Now I'm way too slow to reach my goal.*

At the finish line, 41 minutes after I started, I heard an official explain that the one-mile point was mismarked and short. I learned a new lesson: *listen to your body, not the time.* I vowed that from then on a watch would not govern my pace; it would just keep score on how fast I was running. For my next 10-km race, six months later, I didn't wear a watch and easily broke 40 minutes

Gradually my training runs got faster and longer. In the next couple of years I ran ten miles, and then a half-marathon (13.1-miles). As the distance increased, I finished higher in the pack. *Maybe distance is my friend.* The next step was big and inevitable: a marathon.

Marathon fever was rampant. When Frank Shorter won the Olympic marathon in 1972, the marathon became the Holy Grail for many runners in this country. The Boston Marathon, the world's oldest annual marathon, dating from 1897, surged in popularity and marathons sprang up everywhere.

A marathon used to be 25 miles, but in the 1908 Olympic Games in London the course was extended to 26 miles, 385 yards so runners could start near Windsor Palace, within view of Queen Alexandra, and finish on a stadium track in front of Her Majesty's Royal Box. The extra 1.2 miles extended the agony of the final miles, as Dorando Pietri so famously discovered when he collapsed on the track within sight of that finish line. In 1921, this longer distance for the marathon became official.

Intimidated by the distance, I learned all I could. I read that resting a few days before the race and eating carbohydrate-rich foods helped your liver and muscles store as much carbohydrate as possible, enough to last 18-20 miles. Then your needle on carbohydrate fuel would approach E and your body would "hit the wall." After that you would mostly use fat, a slower-burning fuel that had to be retrieved from storage, making those last few miles especially hard.

I waited until I was ready to run a marathon, not just finish it. That meant doing long training runs, working up to twenty miles once a week, and figuring out how fast I dared to run. During the race, the trick would be to find the Goldilocks pace—not too hot and not too cold—to stay just above my red line until I crossed the finish line. If I started too slowly, I'd run a slower race than I could; if I went out too fast, I'd run a slower race than I could because the final miles would take me into the breakdown lane.

In my first marathon, in 1979, in Coeur d'Alene, Idaho, I'd followed all the advice I'd read, including "cameling up" (drinking lots of fluids) before the race. (That phrase, incidentally, is based on the misguided notion that camels carry large supplies of water in their humps. Camels actually carry mostly fat in their humps, and when that fat is metabolized to generate energy, a considerable amount of internal water is also generated.) Anyway, fully loaded with liquid and two miles into the race, in a residential area, I had to pee. *What can you do?* I turned sideways to the several hundred runners, faced the folks on their front porch watching the race, and watered their lawn while other runners went past, chuckling.

Feeling better, though a little embarrassed, I soon caught up to a ten-year-old boy running with his father who was yelling at him to go faster so he could set a U.S. marathon record for his age. *Child abuse.*

Fearing the distance, I ran feeling like I was saving something for later. I knew I had to break 2:50 to qualify for the Boston Marathon, but suspected that time was out of reach. In the last couple of miles I drew on what I had saved, closed on a runner, and we spent everything sprinting across the finish line as the digital clock displayed 2:53.

I contracted a serious case of marathon fever. Over the next two years I ran as many as three marathons in five weeks and lowered my time by 11 minutes. I knew I was now running the distance about as fast as I could. My running career had reached its summit and was complete. All that was left was to see if I could slightly improve my best times at the distances I had run.

One day I sat down in an easy chair at our public library and picked up a magazine with a picture of a runner on the cover. What came next was a shock.

Inside *Outside* magazine was a story about people running a 100-mile race on trails in California. The race, called the Western States Endurance Run, was born in 1974 from the Tevis Cup, a

100-mile endurance horse race. That year one of the riders, Gordy Ainsleigh, had a horse come up lame and decided to see if he could run the course and finish within 24 hours, the time limit for horses. Remarkably, he did, and he received the same 24-hour belt buckle awarded to Tevis Cup finishers. A new kind of footrace—100 miles on mountain trails—was born.

One hundred miles is an outrageous distance to run. Stored carbohydrate is gone by twenty miles, though even the skinniest person carries enough fat fuel to go 100 miles. But how do you get enough carbohydrate into your bloodstream so your brain keeps working? And how can you take in enough salt, water and fuel during the run so your muscles keep working and not cramp in the California heat? Training for a marathon is very hard; how can you possibly train your body to go nearly four times as far?

The physical and mental challenges electrified me. The day I read that article was the day I wanted to run Western States. I read all I could, started running on hilly trails near home, and made my long runs longer. The next two years I applied to get into Western States and was turned down, each time being told the race was already full. Then I learned why: after each year's run, people immediately signed up for the following year's run, filling the field.

I wrote to the organizers, asking whether they would consider finding a way to let new runners into the race, at least eventually.

The next year they announced a lottery system, with applicants guaranteed entry the third year if they lost in the lottery two consecutive years. My name was drawn in the first lottery.

Be careful what you wish for. Now I have to face the monster.

But two years of waiting had given me time to build endurance and enter the world of ultramarathons—distances longer than a marathon. Each week I was running 70-80 miles, including a long (25-miles or so) trail run, and, to improve my speed, an interval workout running six half-mile pieces as hard as I could on a track.

I ran two 50-mile races on pavement at an average pace of 7:20 per mile. Even so, Western States—100 miles on trails, running up and down in mountain snow and canyon heat, and running through the night using a flashlight—was a different animal altogether. That's twice as far and would take three to four times as long.

As race day approached, late in June, 1983, I drove to Reno with Laurae and our young son, Jedd. The day before the race we drove to nearby Squaw Valley, California, site of the 1960 Winter Olympics, to check in. My blood pressure was too high to meet their requirements, so the nurse, knowing I was just too excited, kindly smiled and told me to go away and sit in a quiet place for a few minutes. When I returned, my blood pressure was acceptable. She wrote my weight and blood pressure on a medical bracelet and attached it to my wrist. I would have to show that bracelet at each medical checkpoint during the race.

Ultrarunners, by and large, are a relaxed, low-key lot. But the Western States prerace meeting is as close as ultrarunning gets to glamour. Star runners and winners of past races were introduced. Others looked like stars in their fine outfits. California glitz was on full display, and my 10-km shirt clearly didn't cut it. I looked at Laurae and Jedd and shook my head. *What made me think I could do this?*

Very early the next day—race day—I slipped away from our motel in Reno to eat breakfast alone. The waitress watched me eat and then slather myself with Vaseline in all the—ahem— necessary places. When I slid off the now-greasy booth, she asked me to leave. I returned to our motel, woke up Laurae and Jedd, and we drove the winding road to Squaw Valley in the pre- dawn darkness. As we pulled into the parking lot, Jedd vomited all over the front seat.

Feeling guilty, I had to leave them as the 5 a.m. start approached. To protect against the eventual sun, I wore a white dress shirt that would never quite be white again. A quart water bottle was cleverly tucked into a holster (latched around my waist by a belt) that originally held bedroom slippers. As I neared the starting line the holster broke. I dumped the whole contraption in a garbage can, knowing I'd now have to carry my bottle loosely in my hand the entire distance. *Maybe I should have practiced this ahead of time.*

The starting gun released 300 runners. We averaged 40-something years old and created a snake of bobbing flashlights leaving the flood-lit starting banner at 6200 feet and ascending switchbacks up a ski slope. Before we finished, we would climb a total of 18,000 feet and descend 23,000 feet, all on trails except for the final two, paved miles into Auburn, a small California town in the center of historic gold country.

Five miles on crusty, five-foot-deep snow brought us atop 8750-foot Emigrant Pass, where we looked back to watch the rising sun showcase Lake Tahoe and the Sierra Mountains. Minor jostling on the next downhill section prompted someone to declare, in a surly voice: "See you suckers on the next uphill."

Ribbons marked the trail, but I just followed the runners ahead of me. After sixteen miles the ribbons disappeared. We were lost. The landscape looked so different with all the snow that even veterans of this race and region couldn't figure out where we were. We fanned out in all directions, looking for ribbons. We came up empty, so our only choice was to back-track until we found ribbons. After 45 lost minutes we found the trail and now struggled in deep snow to pass those at the back of the pack.

Running along the sides of hills on crusty snow was awkward.

A few runners used ski poles to help. Eventually I caught up to Ken Shirk, the second person ever to finish Western States. A muscular celebrity from Hawaii who sometimes donned a headdress of buffalo horns, he called himself "Cowman" because "Cowboy" wasn't sufficient. Briefly within sight of a road, I watched cars pass by him honking while women cheered his name.

At the first aid station where we could meet support people, I searched for Laurae and Jedd. They had expected me sooner and figured they had missed me as all the runners streamed through. But my adventure off course had cost precious time and energy. Finally, just as I was leaving the station, I spotted them and stopped to thank them for being there. After a minute or so I had to say good-bye and run on, knowing it would be many hours before I would see them again.

After thirty miles we reached lower elevation and left the snow behind. One hundred miles is too far to think about, so I just focused on getting to the next aid station (and then the next station), where I could reload my bottle and get food.

Many of the 25 stations had cutoff times; if we arrived there too late, we couldn't continue. A few had drop bags we had filled with food, flashlights, clothing and other items we wanted. We had left those bags—identified by our race numbers—at Squaw Valley yesterday, and they were transported to the stations to be there when we arrived.

Some stations were medical checkpoints. There I would step on a scale and have my weight compared with the prerace weight written on my bracelet. My weight was holding so far, but I knew the rules: if I lost more than 5% of myself I couldn't leave the station until I ate and drank enough to get my loss under 5%; if I lost 7-10%, my bracelet would be cut and removed, ending my race; medical people could also check my blood pressure and anything else if they thought it was necessary, and their decision about letting me continue was final.

We continued running west in remote, rugged terrain following trails used by gold and silver miners in the 1850s. A succession of climbs and canyons took its toll. Near mid-way a tough, one-hour climb brought me to the Devil's Thumb aid station, where I overheard people talking about a nude woman watching us a mile back down the trail. If she was there, I had been too zoned out to notice.

The first runner was expected to finish in about sixteen hours, and the time limit was thirty hours. For many runners, including me, 24 hours was the magic number. Finishers under 24 hours received a silver belt buckle (reflecting the equine origin of the race), while those between 24 and 30 hours received a brass buckle.

As the miles passed and the afternoon got hotter, many

runners stopped at water crossings to soak their bandanas and shirts. After 60 miles, I met Laurae and Jedd again and assured them I could still count to ten and move my legs in a fairly straight line. They encouraged me, helped me with supplies, and then drove off. I asked them to check into our motel in Auburn, get some rest, and meet me at the finish line at 23 hours.

Soon I reached the Foresthill aid station, where pacing could begin. I knew nothing about pacing, but would later learn that pacers are runners who accompany official runners to help them find the course—especially in the dark—and to provide encouragement during the tough, final miles. They are not allowed to carry gear for their runners, and their main purpose is to help keep their runner safe.

Sometimes pacing can go wrong. I learned years later about Jeff, who brought his best friend, Jason—a more accomplished runner—to pace him at Western States. Jason waited patiently all day until Jeff reached Foresthill. By then Jeff was dragging. As they headed down the trail together Jason urged his friend to keep going, and going, but Jeff faded and finally had to drop from the race. Jason, explaining that he hadn't come all the way to California just to run a few miles, then left Jeff and ran the remaining twenty miles by himself, crossing the finish line without his runner. Jeff and Jason never spoke to each other again.

Pacing can also be a very positive experience. Little did I

know that in three future runs at Western States I would twice bring friends to pace me and to introduce them to 100-mile races. But that day—my first time—nobody where I lived had ever run that kind of distance. I ran on from Foresthill alone.

The next aid station, after 74 miles, was White Oak Flats. From its name I had pictured a graceful colonial mansion surrounded by stately trees. Instead, a few trees oversaw a scrubby patch of weeds and berry vines that punctured my legs with bloody scratches as I pondered the sign: "Only A Marathon To Go."

At sunset I reached the American River. A dam ten miles upstream controlled its depth. Some years we could wade across a thigh-high river holding onto a cable and supported by wonderful volunteers who, in shifts, stood in the river all night to ensure no one got swept downstream. With all the snowmelt this year the river was too high, so we were taken across in a motor boat.

Once across I turned on my flashlight, borrowed from someone I had met at our local swimming pool who told me how great it was. When I pointed the light up or down I heard batteries joining or separating as the beam went on or off. *Oops.* The narrow shaft of light pierced the darkening woods, creating snakelike images as the angle of light shifted against sticks, shrubs and rocks. Rustling animal noises and tunnel vision added to the spacey, spooky feeling as I ran at night for the first time.

After a couple of hours, running alone in the middle of the woods, my flashlight died. *I guess I should have practiced running with it. Now what do I do?* I carried no spare flashlight or bulb or batteries, and couldn't tell exactly where the trail was. I groped forward but just couldn't find a ribbon to mark where to go. Stuck in place, I stood for a few minutes with my teeth in my mouth.

Finally two light beams approached from behind. I asked their owners, Skip and his pacer, Jose, if they minded me running right behind them to see the way as best I could. They welcomed me to join them. Now I had not only light but company, something I realized I sorely needed to help take my mind off my aching body. Indeed, my body and mind were at war with each other, my body saying, "I can't go any farther," and my mind replying, "Yes, you can; keep moving."

Nausea engulfed me, probably because my salt/water balance was out of whack. I couldn't look another peanut-butter-and-jelly sandwich in the face. My poor stomach, overloaded from handling so much food and drink all day, went on strike and gave me a choice: drink and throw up, or stop drinking. I chose plan B.

Skip, Jose and I arrived at the final aid station. Six miles to go. Skip wanted to finish in the top twenty because those runners automatically were accepted into next year's run. He was keeping track and knew we were tied for 21st place. A volunteer at the aid station told us the nearest runner left there ten minutes ago and was moving slowly. We gave chase.

We caught and passed the runner, but I was dragging. I told Skip to go ahead and claim 20th place; he seemed stronger than me, and he deserved to finish ahead since I wouldn't have been there without his and Jose's help. After they left, I sagged a bit but struggled on to reach pavement, hike the final hill, and descend into town. With immense satisfaction and relief, I crossed the finish line on the Auburn High School track.

At the finish I didn't see Laurae and Jedd. Then I realized why: I had arrived nearly three hours ahead of the estimate I had given them. I sat in the dark and started shivering. Medical people couldn't find my pulse; I had lost nine pounds, more than 5% of my prerace weight, much of it since I had stopped drinking. If I had weighed this little at an aid station during the race, I wouldn't have been allowed to continue. Now I was so dehydrated that my blood volume was too low to give a pulse. But I was joyfully alive.

While I waited, someone noticed me shaking and kindly put me in a sleeping bag near the finish line. I watched one runner finish and be treated by a podiatrist who snapped pictures of the amazing blisters to show his students. Another, totally spent, had to be lifted two inches onto a bathroom scale to be weighed. For most finishers, though, elation trumped fatigue.

Laurae and Jedd arrived, bundled me off to our motel, and plied me with nibbles of saltine crackers and sips of 7-Up to treat my nausea. The next morning I woke up to a surprise. My energy level was zero, but I was no more stiff and sore than after running a marathon. *Maybe running on trails, mixing running with walking, and changing the muscles as the terrain goes up and down, even for 100 miles, doesn't pound the body as much as running a marathon on pavement does.*

That afternoon we attended a picnic and received our belt buckles. Lining up to receive our awards in order of finish, I stood next to Skip and again thanked him for his and Jose's help last night. Earlier, when I had looked for them, I quickly realized I had no idea what they looked like since we had spent all our time together in the dark.

Later Western States officials discovered that the course was about six miles short, so they lengthened it for future runs. I could only wonder whether I, like Dorando Pietri, would have fallen short (literally) if I'd had to run the extra distance.

4 THE RACE ACROSS THE SKY

Two years after I finished Western States, the doctor said: "You have a decision to make. If we radiate your back, the treatments will probably kill whatever cancer is left, but it will also destroy some lung tissue. You'll never run competitively again."

One year earlier I learned I had testicular cancer. When the doctor said the *C* word, I immediately thought about a long-ago conversation with Barry, who had just finished Harvard Medical School and was doing his medical residency at The Ohio State University when he learned he had an aggressive, untreatable form of cancer. He told me: "At first I thought: Why me? But soon I changed the question to: Why not me? Why should I think I'm so special that I should be exempt from getting a disease that so many other people get?"

Barry's words stayed deep inside me as I underwent surgery and then six weeks of radiation treatments, after which the doctor looked at a clear CT scan and said, "You're cured." I thanked him but knew deep down that he couldn't say those words. What he should have said is that if any cancer remained, it was too tiny to show up on a CT scan.

Now the cancer was back—in my back. Doctors had to thread a needle through my back and into the tumor to get a sample and make the diagnosis. A tumor board in Seattle considered my case and the best means of treatment. Radiologists on that board recommended radiation; chemotherapists recommended chemotherapy. The decision was up to me.

Since the cancer had spread, I chose chemotherapy, which, unlike radiation, treated cancer throughout the body. I'd heard chemotherapy was hard, but how hard could it be? I was tough; I could run 100 miles.

I checked into a hospital in Yakima, where I would stay for five days, receiving daily infusions of the drug combination through the needle in my arm. The plan was for me to undergo four of these five-day treatments, each series separated by me spending two to three weeks at home to recover enough to tolerate the next round.

The first week of treatment wasn't too bad, though each evening, when I knew the drugs were going inside me, I felt queasy and felt my body getting weaker. Each new treatment cycle became harder to handle. Before the fourth and final cycle, I asked my oncologist if I really had to do one more round. He replied: "There's a good chance the cancer is gone. But all the statistical data are based on patients who receive the full dosage of treatment. If it were me, I'd try to make it through the final round."

I checked into the hospital for the final week of treatments. Honestly, those days weren't worth living; their only justification was to get me to days that would be worth living. I survived the worst days by looking at the clock in my room and figuring out how to get through five more minutes, then congratulating myself when I did, and then figuring out how to get through the next five.

To keep some semblance of physical fitness, I walked up and down the hall of the cancer ward, towing the stand connected by the IV needle in my arm, looking at stacked trays of uneaten food and trying not to gag. During one walk, I met an attendant pushing a gurney down the hall carrying the body of a cancer patient who hadn't made it.

I woke up each morning looking at clumps of hair on my pillow. I looked over at my roommate, who was sporting a luxurious head of hair, and asked him how he did it. He smiled and said: "I bought this from the same place that makes them for Donny Osmond. "

I knew, in that instant, that I wouldn't be looking for a hairpiece.

Plagued by nausea the first three rounds, despite the anti-nausea medications I was taking, I looked in desperation for something else to help during the final round. Since marijuana was supposed to reduce nausea, I tried to obtain some. Going through official channels would take too long, a nurse explained, but she obtained some illegally for me. I told my doctor I was doing this, and sprinkled the dry leaves into one of the only foods I could tolerate—apple sauce. It helped.

Back at home, receiving loving care from Laurae and trying to recover from treatment, I was pale and hairless. When I was finally able to spend short times outside, a couple of long-time acquaintances walked right past me on the street without recognizing me.

One night I suddenly craved a Diet Coke. I walked a block, bought one, and guzzled it, enjoying its taste immensely. When I went to bed I discovered that, having not had Diet Coke for many months, its caffeine had an electric effect on me. I spent all night wide awake, my imagination flying me to amazing, interesting places. I had a wonderful time, and the lost sleep was no problem because I wasn't going to be doing much the next day anyway.

Two months after I finished chemotherapy, the radiologist explained that maybe those treatments killed all the cancer; maybe not. Did I want to add another month of radiation treatments to snuff out whatever might be left, even if it meant damaging enough lung tissue that I couldn't run competitively again?

My friends would smilingly tell me I never was competitive. But two months before the cancer was first diagnosed I had finished fifth in my second 100-mile trail race, in the Wasatch Mountains of Utah. And the following month, in my first 24-hour track run, I had set a national single-age (42) record for distance.

Still, the radiologist's question was easy to answer. When you know you might die, things quickly get stripped down to what really matters. There's no point kidding yourself, or anyone else. My life—especially my family and, yes, work—was more important than running. Therefore, I would get the radiation treatments.

At the same time, I didn't entirely believe the radiologist. I believed he was simply telling me the worst-case scenario, something a conscientious physician has to do. I immediately thought about the high-altitude, 100-mile trail run in Leadville, Colorado. *When I get through with my treatments and can run again, I'm going to Leadville and find out what my lungs can handle.*

Three years later, in 1988, Lary (with one *r*) Webster and Bob Thomas, two running friends from Seattle, invited me to join them to take on "The Race across the Sky" in two-mile-high Leadville, the highest incorporated city in the U.S. We would arrive two weeks early to get used to the altitude and scout out the course.

Lary, an engineer at Boeing and, briefly, a professional bowler, was an outstanding road racer. Shortly after he turned fifty, he ran a marathon in a spectacular 2:39. But he'd had trouble with 100-mile trail runs. He had fire in his eyes to complete this one because last year at Leadville he had dropped out after sixty miles, thoroughly chilled by the all-day rain.

I didn't know Bob very well; about all I knew was that he called his girl friend by the name of where she worked: Safeway. He had done some long runs, though never 100 miles, and wasn't optimistic about finishing. But he was tough.

Our adventure began when Lary and Bob piled into my car and we drove away from Ellensburg. The night before Lary and Bob had dined at an all-you-can eat place in town and were feeling the effects. In the middle of nowhere, Bob, turning green, alerted me that his stomach was about to erupt. I quickly pulled to the side of the road and we walked into a field where Bob, to my eyes, set a new world record for volume vomited. That night, after 700 miles, we reached Ogden, Utah and claimed a motel room. I worked out, running round and round in the dark on an elementary school playground, scarcely able to see a thing.

The next day an easy, 480-mile drive brought us into Leadville. We checked into our motel a few miles out of town and then headed to Pizza Hut. Our meal was delayed while restaurant workers attended to a nine-year-old girl who had passed out. "It's the altitude (10,150 feet)," a worker explained. "It happens all the time."

After supper, I ran ten miles in the dark back to our motel, re-tasting spaghetti every step of the way. After one block, my mouth was dry and I thought of a friend who told me that running here was like running at Western States with a sock in your mouth. Still, my first run at high altitude was surprisingly comfortable. *This race is going to be a piece of cake.*

In the morning we began our reconnaissance mission. Lary, Bob (still slightly green from his gastric misadventure two days ago) and I headed out for an easy hike/jog of ninety minutes to explore the first and last (since the race is on an out-and-back course) major climb, Sugarloaf Pass. Lary, the race veteran, couldn't find where to start. We spent most of our time bushwhacking, and it was touch-and-go at the end as we searched side road after side road before finally finding where I had parked my car.

Our ninety-minute workout took four hours, very little of it on course, but we'd learned lots of places *not* to go. *We'll get our act together tomorrow.*

The next morning, in our motel room, Bob cooked pancakes, a preview of our prerace meal. Lary and I glanced dubiously at each other as we tried Bob's product, which was black on the outside and gooey on the inside. A light bulb went on: cooking at high altitude is different from at sea level. We salvaged the meal by switching to plan B: Eggos.

We explored a gentler section of the course. Bob ran well and Lary was full of energy. They disappeared from sight as I dawdled along the gravel road. Altitude was still no problem except when I tried to drink while running; my throat was so busy gulping air that it didn't have room for water, too.

That day I tried a different way to carry gear on the run—a leather belt with a pouch dangling in back. After the run I discovered a brown racing stripe around my waist and a left buttock pink from being spanked on each stride. *End of experiment.*

On the Saturday one week before the race we joined Joe Campbell, a friend from Portland, Oregon, for our last long training run. Late in the afternoon we ran nine miles on trails, over a peak and down into Twin Lakes, at 9200 feet the lowest point on the race course. We enjoyed pie and coffee at a local inn and watched the sun set as Lary pointed out the nearby shed where he had sat shivering for three hours after dropping out of last year's race.

We pulled out our flashlights and warm clothes for the return trip. The night was beautiful, with zillions of stars splattered across the vast heavens. We were doing this to learn more about the race course, but running gently across the trails with friends on a night like this in such a beautiful place was something I'd do anytime and for any reason. Sheer pleasure.

Sunday morning I woke up and searched my body for tread marks from the truck that had apparently run me over while I slept. Finding none, I left Lary and Bob and wobbled into town to go to church. After the service, I stepped outside and met a young man who pointed out the dozen or so 14,000-foot peaks around us. Colorado has 53 in all.

He told me that Leadville, a century ago, had 60,000 residents to mine silver, gold, lead and mostly molybdenum. What we saw now was a shell of what once was—a remnant town of 4000 people making a comeback based on tourism. The last mine (molybdenum) had closed in 1982, removing 3200 jobs and leaving an unemployment rate of 26%. There was no job here for him, recently graduated with a degree in engineering, so he was moving to California.

That afternoon Lary, Bob and I took an easy hike on the trail. I noticed a runner nearby with tight pink shorts and a very smooth running style. Bob recognized him as Frank Shorter, former Olympic marathon champion, who would help cover the race for NBC. For some reason, Frank didn't recognize us.

Monday was a bad day. For three days my ears, nose and throat had been threatening to erupt into something serious. At the same time, I was cutting back on carbohydrates to empty the amount stored in my body before I reloaded.

Not the best of circumstances to hike up one of the most feared places in U.S. trail running—12,600-foot Hope Pass, which sat astride the 45-mile and (after going down the back side and coming back up) 55-mile points of the race. I struggled up the 3400-foot climb in slow motion, far behind Bob and Lary. Two other runners, also checking out the course, passed me, looking good. *What am I doing here?*

I gasped for air, not caring about anything except getting this stupid hike over with. Lary and Bob patiently waited for me at the summit, savoring the spectacular views of snow-capped mountains, green valleys, wildflowers, and rugged rock formations on a picture-perfect day. I finally joined them on top. Since Search and Rescue didn't arrive to carry me out, I staggered back down the hill.

That night we stared at Hope Pass from outside our motel room. It was the low point on the horizon and looked so easy. We retired to our motel lounge to watch the only TV set in the building. Usually the place was packed with early-arriving runners gathering to watch sports or tapes of earlier Leadville runs. But tonight no one was there. When we turned on the set we discovered why: all three stations were covering the Republican national convention.

The next morning Bob perked up. He had been studying race

statistics from previous years and for the first time thought he had a chance to finish. I, on the other hand, felt awful. It hurt to move anything. My resting pulse was 25 beats per minute higher than normal, evidence I overdid it yesterday. I had four days to do nothing but lie around and hope to recover, but for the first time I wondered if I would finish the race

We ate breakfast—frozen waffles that tasted like their cardboard container. Lary and Bob went into town, but I lay in bed all day. That night my pulse was 30 beats per minute above normal. I ached all over and figured it was the flu or some kind of altitude sickness. *If this doesn't end by tomorrow I'm out of the race; I'll crew for Lary and Bob instead.* I said a prayer, asking that Lary and Bob wouldn't get my bug. I could accept not running, but I didn't want to ruin their races.

At daybreak I woke up in sheets drenched with sweat, feeling a little better, my pulse only 19 over normal. I told Lary and Bob they just lost their crew. But Bob was subdued. He had been plagued by sinus trouble and nosebleeds ever since we had arrived, probably caused by altitude. Lary, in contrast, had been healthy and cheerful the whole time, looking forward to his rematch with the course.

Our telephone rang. Someone filming the run asked me, "Can you meet us to do an interview? We'd also like to talk with you during the run, if you don't mind. Your bout with cancer makes you a good human-interest story."

"Okay."

As race day approached, our motel filled with runners. We talked with two of the best-known women runners. Kathy D'Onofrio-Wood, 23, was a pixie, redheaded art student with a high, squeaky voice who finished second woman here last year and could run most of us into the ground. Helen Klein was here for her third 100-mile trail run of the year, with two more to go. You'd never guess she was 65 years old.

We met Randy Spears, who had come out a month early to prepare for the run. Eleven of his friends and relatives, complete with matching, specially-designed T-shirts, arrived from Texas to crew and pace him. Indeed, many runners had crew and pacers along to help. Lary, Bob and I were flying solo.

Two days before the race, we woke up to a crisp, sunny morning that had chased away the rain and mist of the last two days. Outside our motel cows grazed in a meadow against a backdrop of Mt. Elbert, Colorado's highest peak at 14,433 feet, gleaming with a fresh dusting of snow. Cabin fever reached epic proportions as Bob, Lary and I vied for the chance to cook, wash dishes, make beds, anything.

We drove into town to watch the Coors International Bike Classic. After an hour of standing around, waiting on a street corner, listening to speculation about how soon they would be arriving, we watched the bikers flash by in less than one minute. I imagined Peggy Lee singing: "Is That All There Is?"

That evening all the runners, crews and pacers assembled for the first time in an auditorium. We checked in, ate dinner and heard from the event organizers—Merilee O'Neal and Ken Chlouber, who gave an inspiring prerace talk, exhorting us to remember, "You're tougher than you think you are and you can do more than you think you can."

Reflecting the town's mining heritage, Ken presented the Jackass Award to Essie Garrett, who had gotten lost on the course each of the previous two years. Last year she had pulled leaves over herself at night to keep warm. She was back to try again.

The day before the race we received a medical check and had hospital bracelets with our vital statistics clamped onto our wrists, where they had to stay until we finished (or were finished by) the race. At this elevation many of us set new records for pulse and blood pressure.

We made our final guesses about what gear to leave in which drop bags and turned them in, knowing they would be waiting for us at five of the aid stations on the course. We went to Joe Campbell's rented house for spaghetti, grape juice and bread. *The last supper.*

Restaurants were open early on race day and teeming with customers. At 4 a.m. 270 runners, armed with flashlights and warm clothes, were ready. Lary, Bob and I wished each other good luck and then disappeared into the darkness. For some reason—maybe my recent flu, or whatever it was—I didn't feel strong heading downhill on pavement. A few miles later our lights bobbed as we formed a conga line on the trail along Turquoise Lake, running past sleeping campers.

I was already twenty minutes behind schedule as the sun rose and we reached the first aid station, thirteen miles in, where we were greeted and helped by women dressed as saloon floozies. My schedule was based on trying to finish in less than 25 hours, the standard here for earning a huge silver and gold belt buckle. Later finishers who beat the 30-hour time limit would receive a silver buckle.

On the long climb up Sugarloaf Pass I was in 175th place, finally catching up with Essie Garrett. In some secluded bushes my breakfast flew out of my mouth. The aid station at 21 miles came 45 minutes behind my schedule. At least I was following the third part of the ultrarunner adage: eat like a horse; drink like a fish; and run like a turtle.

At 30 miles, on a dirt road, I moved up to fifth place among the six Washington runners I knew here. At 41 miles, one mile after refueling at the Twin Lakes aid station, we cross a small river. I had carefully planned how to keep my feet dry here to prevent later blisters: walk across in no shoes and an old pair of socks, carrying dry socks and shoes to put on when I was across.

That part worked fine. But once across, I discovered that I had left my freshly filled water bottles on the other side when I took off my shoes to carry them. A race official saw my dilemma and kindly offered to toss the bottles over to me. His first toss was short, and all the water came out when the bottle bounced on the ground. The official kindly carried the second bottle across to me.

Now I faced the long climb up Hope Pass without enough water. But I remembered, from the endless hike here a week ago, that the trail eventually goes along a stream. The good news is that at the first opportunity I filled my bottles. The bad news is that while doing so, I slipped on a wet stone and into the stream. *So much for keeping my feet dry. I hope this water is safe to drink. But if it isn't, at least I'll be done with this run before the Giardia fully infect me.*

The ascent up Hope Pass was tough, so I gave the climb its due. Slow and steady. Near the summit I caught up with Bob, who, like me, was grouchy and uncertain he'd finish. Just before the crest, at 45 miles, the two race leaders passed by going the other direction (55 miles for them). They were singing. *At least I can sing better than them.*

The aid station on top provided supplies carried up by llamas now basking in sunlight. I caught my breath, enjoyed the panoramic view, ran down the back side, and jogged the road into Winfield, a ghost town that marked 50 miles. I was far behind the 25-hour schedule, but felt good enough to begin the 50-mile return trip.

On the dreaded climb back up Hope Pass, I caught up to the runner who held the U.S. women's record for a 50-mile road run. We got acquainted and headed up together. Being a gentleman, I let her go first. The only problem was that she, like many people at high altitude, had the unfortunate tendency to pass gas. She kept apologizing, offering to let me take the lead, but I didn't want to asphyxiate her, either.

We took our sweet time. I was determined to reach the summit with something left and not spend everything on the climb. It worked like magic. Once on top I wished her luck and tore down the other side, suddenly feeling good. The only sad point was when I passed Lary, who was struggling and would be delayed at the next medical checkpoint because of low blood pressure—the same place where last year he dropped out of this race. I wished him the best and ran on, this time blasting across the river and into the aid station at Twin Lakes (60 miles).

I talked to the TV cameras for a couple minutes and borrowed a flashlight from a friend who had passed out atop Hope Pass and had been revived with oxygen canisters. He had dropped out of the race, but his flashlight saved me because mine was in my drop bag at the next aid station, which I wouldn't reach until well after dark.

As I left Twin Lakes at dusk and ascended the next hill, I heard an explosion and felt stickiness on my hand. I discovered my fresh supply of Coke had blown the cap off my bottle, leaving me with just one bottle to cover the next two hours. But I didn't care. Nearing the summit, I was on top of the world where the stars were shining and the trees were glowing, giving a spiritual, other-worldly aura to the trail that I later learned was foxfire—a phosphorescent glow emitted from fungi in rotting wood. The night was magical, and by the next aid station, visions of the big belt buckle were dancing in my head.

With twenty miles to go, I was running high on hope but low on energy. Going back up Sugarloaf Pass, mostly walking, was hard. Following a flashlight beam for hours, with shadows darting about as the angles changed on objects, with rustling noises all around in the woods (I didn't want to know what they were), I felt spacey. The trail seemed to go on forever as I reached the final aid station.

Thirteen miles to go. The cancer survivor talked briefly to the cameras, referring to his journey through the valley of the shadow of death. Then he headed for home.

The final three hours he didn't see another runner; not even a flashlight beam. Along Turquoise Lake, then finally onto pavement that brought him back into Leadville. To his final camera he said a few words for his wife, Laurae. That day was their 22nd wedding anniversary.

Forty-six minutes before the 25-hour mark, I became the 35th finisher. The banner didn't just mark the finish line; it marked my return to health after cancer. To me it said: *"Welcome Back; You're Whole Again."*

I rested in the medical tent to regroup and watch other people finish. Joe had already finished, number 20. Finisher 49 was Lary Webster. We grinned and headed off to our motel to shower, not knowing how Bob was doing. Slightly refreshed, we returned to the finish line to greet others. Then we drove onto the paved part of course to check on Bob.

We celebrated when we met Bob three miles from the finish line. He carried a smile a mile wide under nostrils encrusted with blood. For the last thirty miles, he'd been plugging his nose with Kleenex to stop the flow. Soon he became finisher number 86. We three joined a large crowd watching as the clock ticked down. Six minutes before the 30-hour time limit expired, the final finisher, Essie Garrett, crossed the line to a huge ovation.

Thanks to perfect weather, half of those who started the race finished it. The finishing rate for the three men in Room 45 at our motel, however, was 100%. As we got into the car the next day to drive home, Lary reached for the road atlas and asked with a smile, "What state are we in?"

The answer was obvious: Euphoria.

5 WONDERLAND

When they go well, races are dessert for all your hard training. You feel extra strong and fast, and most of the race is sheer fun. In the early miles, you feel like you could just take off and leave nearby runners behind if you wanted to. You feel as close to invincible as you're going to get.

And when a race goes badly, you learn new lessons. *Did you try to run too fast, especially at the start? How does your training need to be improved? How can you better take care of your feet and your stomach?* After every race, I wrote in my diary what I'd learned and what I'll do differently next time.

Maybe 25% of your performance in a long race depends on your health that day and how well you handle conditions during the race—weather, food, drink, clothing, pace, staying on course, attitude, dealing with medical problems. The other 75% comes from your genetics and training. Juma Ikangaa, a Tanzanian runner who finished second three years in a row at the Boston Marathon, famously explained: "The will to win means nothing without the will to prepare."

Maybe after cancer I'm wasn't a competitive runner any more, but Leadville showed me I could still run. My competitive spirit hadn't changed; I still wanted to be the best I could be. To find out how good you can be, though, you have to test yourself in races. So I kept racing at distances from 5 km to 100+ miles. Once in a blue moon, when no elite runners showed up, I would finish first.

I loved racing, but then I discovered it wasn't the only kind of dessert you could have when you are in good running shape. I learned that when I was invited by Karen and Mark Clement, two accomplished distance runners from Oregon, to join their friends to run around Mt. Rainier on the Wonderland Trail. I eagerly accepted.

This was definitely not a race. The idea was to cover about one-third of the trail each day, taking time to enjoy the magnificent scenery and literally smell the flowers. Karen and Mark arranged for everyone's camping gear to be transported each day to the next campsite, so all we had to do was carry a light pack with food and drink and enjoy ourselves.

I discovered I could have a whole new set of adventures: running in challenging, beautiful and interesting places, on my own or with like-minded friends. I should have realized this sooner because I'd read about ultrarunners crossing the United

States west to east on pavement, and south to north on the Appalachian, Pacific Crest and Continental Divide trails. Later I would read about a very few people running across Canada, around Australia, or even across the Sahara Desert.

Most adventure runs, though, are a day or two in beautiful places such as national parks. I was lucky to have one nearly in my back yard where, thanks to Karen and Mark, I'd get to play.

Mount Rainier is the crown jewel of Washington state. Her year-round coat of snow, fortified annually with as much as 1000 inches of new whiteness, gleams in the sunlight. At 14,411 feet, the most prominent and glaciated peak in the lower 48 states, and the tallest peak from base to summit, she majestically presides over all other peaks in the Cascade Mountain Range. One of the most-climbed mountains in the country, her crevasses and weather annually turn back nearly half of her 10,000 suitors.

Not everyone comes to climb her; many just want to look at her. One of the best places to do this, where you can see her up close and from every angle, is on the Wonderland Trail, a 93-mile path that encircles her at elevations ranging from 2320 to 6750 feet. Late summer is the only time you can go all the way around without crossing major snow fields.

Backpackers typically hike the trail in ten to fourteen days. With total ascents and descents of 27,000 feet each, you are almost always going up or down. The fastest known supported run on the whole trail is 20 hours and change; the fastest unsupported run is a touch under 29 hours. But no official records exist, because you aren't allowed to have races in national parks.

Karen and Mark started their three-day runs around the mountain, always in August, in the early 1980s. One year a Washington runner described the experience in *UltraRunning*, the flagship magazine for ultrarunners. He said the Oregon runners, whose highest state peak is 11,240-foot Mt. Hood, had "mountain envy" going around Mt.Rainier. A chill ensued, and for a few years the Oregon and Washington runners made separate expeditions around the mountain, sometimes meeting each other running the same week-end, going in opposite directions. Eventually peace was restored.

Mt. Rainier is where I forged friendships with many ultrarunners, including three—Lary, Bob and Joe—who ran at Leadville with me. Those friendships developed because we shared a love for the sport and spent lots of time together on the trail and around the campfire at the end of each day.

Mt. Rainier is also where I met people who liked to run around other nearby mountains. Those friendships would lead to other, one- or two-day expeditions around Mt. Hood, Mt. St. Helens and Mt. Adams. A whole new world opened up to me.

<u>The Night Before</u> Mid-afternoon I drove into Mt. Rainier National Park and pulled into the registration area at Cougar Rock Campground, a few miles from where we would start running the next day. A note on a pie plate tacked onto the board told me which group site was ours. I found the place and saw a couple of vehicles attached to trailers. I spotted who I assumed were the Clements and introduced myself.

Karen, an effusive, white-haired high school science teacher who had finished Western States, immediately welcomed me and, with a big smile, took me under her wing and showed me where to set up my tent. Mark, who had dark hair, a sturdy frame, and worked for a computing company was a little more reserved but readily came over and helped me feel welcome, knowing I was largely among strangers.

As daylight faded, the invited runners—about twenty in all including three women—continued to trickle in from all directions, giving me a chance to put faces to names I had read about.

That night Mark gathered us around a large, detailed map of the mountain and gave a trail briefing, describing tomorrow's section. We would break camp early, drive to the Longmire Visitor Center, park our cars there and leave promptly at 7 a.m. We could run with anyone we chose and take all the time we wanted, but no one was to run alone.

Mark was like a mother hen, very concerned about our safety and strict about only invited runners being in our group. One of the runners, Lary Webster, wondered why Mark was so worried about us. After all, we were all competent and experienced runners; if we weren't, we wouldn't have been invited. Many years later, after he organized the Rainier run himself, Lary would say: "I finally know how Mark felt. You can't know how responsible you feel unless you've done this. If anything bad happened to any of the runners I invited, I'd feel terrible about it. I'd also wonder if I could get into legal trouble."

Longmire to Mowich Lake The next morning we rose early and packed our camping gear into trailers that would travel north to Mowich Lake, our destination for the night. We drove to Longmire, the southwest entrance to the national park that was our starting point, and our finish line in three days.

Some years we ran the Wonderland Trail counterclockwise; sometimes we ran it clockwise, the direction I describe here. In the clockwise years, the first day was the hardest: 34 miles with a net gain of 2000 feet; five big climbs and four descents. (Going counterclockwise, of course, put this section on the final day, when we were more tired, but reversed the number of ascents and descents, giving us a net *descent* of 2000 feet.)

My first year, as a newbie, I just followed the leaders.

Promptly at 7 a.m., with whoops and hollers, we jogged out of the parking lot at Longmire and onto a trail. I followed some veterans running uphill in a forest. In overgrown sections, the plants painted our bodies with morning dew. Within an hour, as our adrenalin subsided, we ran less and hiked more. We were fresh, excited and eager to catch up on each other's news. I didn't know many of the runners and didn't have many stories to tell, so I mostly listened and learned.

Mark had stressed that this wasn't a race, but it was hard to stifle our competitive juices. I wanted to show, at least myself, that I could keep up with some people I knew were good runners. Finally I decompressed, got with Mark's program, and began to enjoy the magnificent scenery.

It was hard to miss. For more than an hour our trail climbed through forests of Douglas fir and hemlock up to 5500-foot Indian Henry's Hunting Ground, where a ranger cabin nestled in the trees along a meadow festooned with wildflowers. Lary Webster said: "When they blow up the world, this is where I want to be."

We stopped, topped off our water bottles and downed some trail food we carried in fanny packs. Mount Rainier loomed on our right, as she would for three days. The trail continued north, almost always going up or down. We crossed a swaying, 100-foot-high, 250-foot-long suspension bridge staring down—way down—at Tahoma Creek. One runner with acrophobia—a fear of heights—didn't look down. Others held him and helped him and his white knuckles safely across.

As we got spread out, I suddenly found myself all alone (violating one of Mark's rules) heading toward Emerald Ridge, enjoying the beauty of this place. I lost my inhibitions (and common sense) and accepted an earlier challenge by another runner to see how long I could run unseen without wearing shorts. Thirty minutes passed safely. Then around a blind corner I suddenly faced a man and woman hiking my way. I tried simultaneously to zip past them, slip on my shorts and apologize profusely. The man just shook his head and replied, with a tinge of disgust, "No big deal."

He reminded me of the time I ran a 5-km race *au naturel* in a family nudist park. We ran uphill to the boundary of the park and then returned. The course was lined with trees except for the final 50 yards, where a friend of mine, sprinting to the finish line with two other men, was dismayed to hear a voice announce over the loud speaker system: "Here comes a *small* group."

Back to Rainier. The day was long and beautiful. We were running the driest section of trail, but occasionally found places to refill our water bottles. I treated my water with iodine, others used filters, and some veterans just drank straight out of the streams, taking their chances.

Late afternoon we reached the Mowich River, whose

makeshift bridges were washed away. We walked on rocks and logs and waded where necessary to get across. Our reward was the final, steep, three-mile climb to Mowich Lake Campground. John, our oldest runner, lingered at the bottom while his heart palpitated and Mark, on top, worried about his friend's safety. John eventually made it up the hill, as we all did.

The final climb extracted its pound of flesh. In a future year, I would spot Mel van Houten, a friend from Ellensburg, in the bushes near his tent at Mowich Lake, throwing up after his climb. By late afternoon everyone had arrived. We retrieved our camping gear from the trailer, set up our tents and took an icy dip in the lake to clean up. Feeling fresher, we dove into our food and drink.

After supper, I joined a group of runners deep in conversation. They explained that they had been talking about how old they were the first time they had sex. I replied that I'd reveal mine if they revealed theirs. The youngest reported ages— 14 being the lowest—came from the women. They oohed in disbelief when I told them my first time was at age 24, on my wedding night.

Mowich Lake to White River The night was nippy at 4929 feet. The next morning we ate, packed our gear into the trailer, and left when we pleased. Day two is the shortest—27 or so miles depending on the route we chose—running east across the north end of the mountain. We could take the official Wonderland route up Ipsut Pass or the longer, more scenic trail through Spray Park.

I just followed the veterans (this is a recording), who headed for Spray Park. After a short detour to see the sights and feel the mist from water plummeting down Spray Falls, we climbed in snow to the top of the park, where we spotted a herd of mountain goats in the distance. Starting the descent, I heard laughter. I joined the fun as we either tried desperately to keep our feet from shooting out in the snow, or we glissaded, collecting as much snow as possible under our shorts.

We crossed Carbon River on a suspension bridge and climbed along Carbon Glacier, hearing and watching chunks of glacier crash into the river. Eventually the trail, destroyed by winter storms, became rough as we followed flagging to mark the new, temporary route.

Late morning brought us to big, open views of Mt. Rainier as we reached Mystic Lake. We sat along the beach to laze in the sun and eat lunch. The gleaming mountain, beautifully reflected in the still lake, suddenly blurred when a couple veterans plunged in to skinny-dip.

After the leisurely break to enjoy ourselves (this is another recording), we resumed running. Rounding the bottom of

Winthrop Glacier, we reached the long, switch-backing climb through the woods to 6700-foot Skyscraper Pass. Now above tree line, I felt the cooler air and a touch of nausea. Sitting down to refuel, my new friends showed me two new (for me) trail elixirs—string cheese and beef jerky. Soon we were running again, the vistas opened up, and we reached another decision point at Frozen Lake.

I took Option A, which was to continue on the Wonderland Trail to the Sunrise Visitor Center. On the way, I met many people—more than I'd seen the entire trip—streaming out from Sunrise on day hikes. I stopped at the Visitor Center to indulge myself in French fries and ice cream, a tasty improvement over my usual camp cuisine consisting of cold food and a heated can of stew.

From Sunrise, the Wonderland Trail plunges 2000 feet in three miles, bringing us to our destination for the night, White River Campground. Mark Clement invited me to race him there, apparently forgetting that "this is not a race." I declined, explaining that I needed to save my strength for the final day. But I didn't tell him the other reason: I'd heard (correctly) that he was an absolute terror running downhill.

In a future year, at Frozen Lake, I would take Option B, which was prettier and longer. There we took a different trail south, going straight at the majestic mountain, getting as close to it as possible. Snow depth determined how far we could go on Burroughs Mountain, where on a fine day we could look across a chasm and see people climbing toward the summit of Mt. Rainier. Marmots whistled while chipmunks scampered over nearby rocks, trying to filch our trail food. Once we'd had our fill of eye candy, we'd run a rugged trail down to White River Campground.

During the afternoon, runners taking either option trickled into camp and enjoyed the luxury of bathrooms with running water. Our final night featured a pajama party, a costume contest and initiation of rookies, who had to see how long they could sit in the milky, glacier-fed White River. Few, including me, could last one minute, and women generally outlasted the men.

After the initiation ritual, a few years later, I would hear stories around the campfire from a celebrated runner, Susan Gimbel, who won a 100-mile race in her home state of California and was one of the first women to run a double crossing of the Grand Canyon: running down from the South Rim, across the Colorado River, and up the North Rim, and then returning to the South Rim by the same route—nearly 50 miles and all in one day. Once, she even made a quadruple crossing in close to 24 hours.

A lawyer, her day job was to write articles in a legal journal analyzing important cases. She told us many details about the O. J. Simpson trial, which she had observed and written about. "When O. J. struggled to fit his hand into the bloody glove," she said, "the trial was effectively over." She also revealed her favorite trail remedy for nausea: eating ginger. Many of us took note.

I crawled into my tent to rest up for day three. The night was uneventful that first year. But it wasn't always that way.

In a future run, I would camp within earshot of Mike and Sharon, a trim, attractive triathlete with excellent flotation. The night would be punctuated by her excited gasps of "Oh, Michael. Oh, Michael. O God." I wouldn't be the only one losing sleep that night. The next morning, and forever after, Mike would privately be known by his new name: "God."

White River to Longmire We rose early and packed up for the final day. I overheard a sharp exchange between a married couple. Next year they would still be married, but not to each other.

We would run nineteen miles south to Box Canyon, where vehicles were parked, waiting for us. From there we would go west to Longmire, our finish line, either by catching a ride or by running fourteen less scenic miles on trail. Taking a ride at Box Canyon enabled runners to arrive home at a reasonable hour that night, and those who had already completed the Wonderland Trail often chose this option. But stopping short wasn't an option for me the first time; I was excited to do the whole trail.

The route to Box Canyon was, for me, the prettiest of the

entire trip. The trail leaving White River Campground was carpeted with conifer needles. We passed banana slugs like they were standing still, eventually breaking out of a forest and crossing a roaring creek. We zigzagged up along an alpine meadow filled with lupines, frequently crossing a meandering stream. A chunk of bear scat on the trail was accompanied by a piece of toilet paper left by some joker ahead of us.

The climb passed by Summerland, a beautiful camp near a 360-degree vantage point. Immediately west was Mt. Rainier in all its glory. Low on its flank was Mark, who had hiked there earlier in the morning. He kept climbing a snowy section and sliding back down, yelling and being a kid again. To the east, a herd of mountain goats frolicked. Mt. St. Helens and Mt. Adams peeked over the southern horizon and smiled at us while the lovely meadow we just passed lay north.

We hiked in snow to the highest point on the Wonderland Trail, 6750-foot Panhandle Gap. Here we had to be careful. I don't have acrophobia, but I am a bit leery of sharp drop-offs. I edged toward the summit, staring once at the steep, snowy hill that fell away sharply on my right and the rugged rocks at the bottom waiting to painfully terminate any slide if I slipped. I concentrated on looking straight ahead, carefully placing each footstep.

Once on top, we searched for cairns to guide us through the

snow for the next mile or two. Then the trail became visible and started descending into Indian Bar. Snow gradually gave way to a riot of wildflowers, starring magenta paintbrush, in this Sound of Music place. We ran down to the Bar, where a stone shelter sat behind a bridge crossing a clear, rushing creek. *When they blow up the world, this is where I want to be.*

We lingered there, having a bite to eat and reloading our bottles from the creek. Then we moved on with regret, knowing the best scenery was behind us. A forest of giant old-growth cedar and fir awaited us as the trail undulated for several miles along the Cowlitz Divide before diving down into Box Canyon.

We began the descent. In a future year, this is where Steve Varga, a friend from Ellensburg, said he needed to take a short pit stop. I told him I'd just walk ahead until he caught up. But once he disappeared into the trees, I ran as hard as I could to Box Canyon. When he arrived there, he had blood in his eyes. Other runners, waiting in the parking lot to catch their rides to Longmire, watched in amazement as Steve, a high school wrestler, charged across the lot to put his patented takedown move on me.

The first year, I took no ride at Box Canyon. I refueled and ran onto a path through ordinary forest scenery that alternated between dusty and overgrown. Nearing the last major climb in Stevens Canyon, I was startled by a wild scream. Suddenly a runner I knew, minus his shorts, shot past me and charged up the hill as the sun glinted off his white, skinny butt.

The climb was long, especially on tired legs, and finally topped out at picturesque Reflection Lakes. My lumbering legs carried me briefly onto pavement and then onto trail and a short, scenic detour to Narada Falls. Near the end, running through dusty forestland, I met a troop of Boy Scouts carrying heavy packs and glum faces. Only their adult leaders looked enthusiastic.

The finish was as anticlimactic as the scenery. The miles ended at Longmire, where I popped out of the woods and into the parking lot. Most of the runners had stopped at Box Canyon and had already left for home. I chatted with the few who remained, cleaned up, retrieved my camping gear, thanked Karen and Mark for my David in Wonderland experience, and plopped into my car to drive home, tired and happy.

6 LEWIS AND CLARK

One year after running Leadville, and newly in love with the Wonderland Trail, I discovered a new adventure waiting on my doorstep. Washington was about to celebrate its 100th anniversary of statehood. As part of the festivities, the Washington State Parks and Recreation Commission decided to organize a run across the state: 500 paved miles, roughly following the route Lewis and Clark took two centuries ago.

During the running renaissance in the 1970s, almost everyone ran on pavement. Compared with trails, paved roads were faster and smoother, more accessible to more people, and easier for organizers to measure distances accurately and get supplies and volunteers to aid stations. Though they were a fringe group, ultrarunners also ran mostly on pavement, typically 50 km (31.1 miles) or 50 miles. European ultrarunners, accustomed to the metric system, sometimes ventured out as far as 100 km.

The tide began to turn for ultrarunners in the late 1970s when the Western States Endurance Run was born. Longer distances seemed possible, and trails offered advantages over pavement: a softer surface; more interesting and challenging surroundings; and runners using different muscle groups as the terrain changed. For ultrarunners, the next three decades brought a slow but steady switch from roads to trails.

Now imagine the Lewis and Clark Trail Run—on pavement. The organizers invited relay teams from around the world to celebrate with an eight-day run across the state. Ten-person teams would cover 50-74 miles a day, with each team member running an average of 10 km a day. The event would be in early April and take runners west along the Columbia River to Cape Disappointment, where Clark famously wrote in his journal in 1805: "Ocian in view! O, the joy!" (What Clark actually saw was the mouth of the Columbia River emptying into the Pacific Ocean. The expedition then spent a miserable winter slightly inland before returning to St. Louis.)

A couple of ultrarunners asked the Commission why the run was only a relay event. Would they also allow solo runners? It seemed barely possible that someone could run 100 km a day for eight straight days, and the idea would add interest to the event, so the organizers agreed to give it a trial run.

One year before the official race, organizers staged a two-day preview run, inviting solo runners to race legs five and six on the course. Twenty-two tried and seven finished both days, with everyone fighting the April headwinds tearing east through the Columbia River Gorge, a place now dotted with wind farms. Runners had so much trouble that it made the decision easy for the organizers: solo runners would be welcome the next year.

Ignorance is bliss. A few of us, none of whom had tried the preview run, started training in earnest for the event. A few months before the race, riding a bus to the start of a run, I overheard a couple runners behind me talking about their experiences fighting the wind during the preview run and laughing at how impossible it would be for anyone to complete the actual race. I silently listened to them, smiling smugly and knowing that I would finish the run across my state.

Multiday runs were *terra incognita* for me, and I knew I'd have to get used to running long distances back-to-back on pavement. On Saturdays I ran an old highway from home to a town 25 miles away, stopped at Safeway for supplies, and then ran back. Sundays were the same. As race day approached, after doing two consecutive 160-mile weeks, I was injured. *Duh.*

The final three weeks gave time for the injuries to heal and to figure out logistics. Laurae, two of her sisters, our daughter, Lindsay, and a family friend would be my support crew and live in a rented motor home. After two days, Lindsay and our friend would leave, but the others would remain for all eight days and accompany me along the course, as race rules permitted. Our team name was Uff Da, a Norwegian expression of dismay at facing a daunting task.

The day before the race we checked in. More than a thousand relay runners, on 140 teams, had come from many states and from as far away as Japan and New Zealand. The mood was festive as we gathered at Lewiston, Idaho, where the race would begin. The thirty ultrarunners were lost in the crowd, an afterthought to the main event.

We solo runners assembled the next morning before sunrise and were sent off alone, running Highway 12 west across the Snake River into Clarkston, Washington and then fifty more miles to Dayton, our destination for the night. One hour later, each day, the relay runners took off, soon shooting past us and yelling encouragement. When they finished, typically by 4 p.m., they would find an all-you-can-eat place or one of the many dinners offered by local groups in the host community. Evening entertainment was arranged by the organizers, so relay runners could go to bed early or party late into the night.

Our small band of ultrarunners—brothers and sisters—faced a strong headwind on day one and soon spread out as Canadian geese watched from nearby grassy cliffs. In the early miles I kept company with Jay Birmingham, asking him about his unsupported, 72-day run from Los Angeles to New York City several years earlier. At the top of a 1400-foot climb, where relay runners passed their batons to their next runner, a portable toilet was blown down. Aid was available there, but solo runners relied on their roving support crews.

About 6 p.m., I ran the final few miles into Dayton with Doug McKeever, a friend and solo runner of similar ability—so similar, in fact, that we had finished just a few minutes apart at Leadville the year before. We met our support teams, bought dinner from a local group, and settled in for a restful night while many of the relay runners drank and danced into the wee hours. *So far, so good.*

The next day we ran 74 miles, the longest leg of the entire event. Feeling a bit stiff and sore, I lined up in the dark for our departure with ten fewer solo runners than on day one. Relay runners passed us earlier than they had the first day, leaving us alone with our support teams after the first few hours. The headwind and wheat fields kept us company as we headed toward the Tri-Cities (Richland, Kennewick and Pasco), where the Yakima, Snake and Columbia Rivers converge.

Late in the day, Doug and I again ran together. He was grumpy about what had happened earlier that day: another solo runner had kept running right behind him to let Doug shield the wind for him, but hadn't returned the favor and taken his turn. We reached our destination well into the night and learned that the remaining solo runners could now proceed in two different ways: run the distance each day specified for the relay teams; or go as you please, completing as much distance as you wanted each day and sleeping whenever and wherever you pleased. Most of us were following the first option, but at least one, Jesse Riley, was walking the entire distance using plan B.

When we assembled in the dark to start day three, only eight runners appeared. After two long days on pavement, neither Doug nor I could run. So we walked. Off we went, with Doug talking about tendons so sore yesterday (from running on the cant of the road) that he had taken an 800-mg dose of ibuprofen to kill the pain and then run too many miles on his damaged legs. The pain was back, but so was he.

Neither of us was a fast walker under the best of conditions. And these definitely weren't the best. Doug wrestled with pain while I tolerated feet that were swollen and blistering despite being wrapped in duct tape. Our support crews brought us burgers and did their best to cheer us on, and we were immensely grateful. But eventually Doug's pain became too great, and after 14 hours and 38 miles he was forced to stop. The next morning, when he tried to resume, he had to crawl to get to the bathroom. His run was over.

I walked all day and into the night without seeing another "runner." Sleeplessness and fatigue took their toll. I wove down the road, pointing my flashlight at telephone poles and counting them. My wonderful crew slept in shifts, keeping someone awake to help me. After 23 hours I reached Crow Butte State Park, near the lovely grounds of the Columbia Crest Winery, and crawled into the motor home to get a pittance of sleep.

One hour later, I was at the starting line for day four with only Ray Nicholl, Adrian Crane, and Steve Frederickson, who was race walking just that day's section. But others were still out there. Jim Thatcher was nearby. Jesse Riley was going well, but keeping to his own schedule and sleeping elsewhere, maybe just ahead of us. And Bobby Wise was somewhere. Stay tuned for their stories.

We left in darkness and I just couldn't keep up. Even walking was painful; each step on pavement hurt my swollen, blistered feet. Cutting open the front of my shoes didn't help enough. The headwind was relentless. I stopped frequently, taking short naps, and doing my best to deserve the great help my crew was giving me.

At least I had a crew. On this day, Jim Thatcher, whose best friend of twenty years was crewing for him, arrived at the place, two miles down the road, where they were to meet. Jim found the vehicle, flashers on, with a note from his friend saying he was tired of crewing and had left.

Bobby Wise, from East Point, Georgia, wasn't faring any better. He was far behind the rest of us, stopping when he wanted and walking when he wanted. The night before a police officer spotted him sleeping under a truck at a service station and asked what he was doing there. Bobby replied that he was doing the Lewis and Clark Trail Run. Not believing him, and seeing no evidence that such a run existed, the officer took him to a mental hospital for observation. Released after a few days, Bobby returned to the service station and resumed (and would eventually complete) his odyssey across the state.

As I trudged along, barely moving, I thought about the woman crossing the finish line at a marathon who heard the voice over the loudspeaker announce: "Here's the first finisher in the walking division."

She screamed back: "I'm not walking."

But I was, all day and through the night, taking short sleep breaks. The next afternoon, totally spent, I passed the Stonehenge replica on a bluff overlooking the Columbia River Gorge. A mile past that monument to local men killed in World War I, I reached Maryhill State Park, the finish point for day four. But I was well into day five.

After 260 miles, I just couldn't go any farther. I showered and cleaned up, trying to figure out what to do next, when Jim Thatcher arrived and got on the phone. He wouldn't finish in eight days, but he was determined to keep going until he did finish.

Jim worked at the state penitentiary in Olympia and had made friendly bets about whether he could finish this run. With a smile, he talked on the phone, renegotiating the wagers at more favorable odds now that he'd lost his support crew. He also called his wife to ask her to come out and crew for him.

I bade Jim farewell, joined my crew, and climbed into our motor home. My race was over, but we had rented the vehicle until the end of the week, and we had cleared our schedules until then. We decided to follow what was left of the race.

The first order of business was to check on Jim. I didn't believe he could keep going with no immediate support. I knew he'd get help when his wife arrived, but could he be getting rides now and then to cover part of the distance? After a couple hours of rest, our merry crew drove west and caught up to Jim, who was walking on the road with no help in sight. I checked on him a couple more times and concluded, with some shame, that my suspicions about him were completely groundless.

A day or two after the event officially ended, Jim crossed the finish line. The next time I saw him, a year later, I would congratulate him on finishing, confess my suspicions, and apologize. He would smile and hand me a vial of sand he collected when he finished at Cape Disappointment.

You might be wondering, though, what would keep runners from getting rides in their support vehicles? After all, no one else would know; race officials and relay runners were nowhere around after the first couple of hours each day, and the few remaining solo runners were far apart; indeed, we were entirely on the honor system.

The answer is that whatever fame and fortune you might get from winning, or even finishing, would be overshadowed by knowing you cheated. Because there is no fame and fortune. Hardly anyone makes a living from ultrarunning, which is about as close to an amateur sport as there is.

We left Jim, whose help was on the way, and drove down the road to see if we could help anyone still in the official race. Ray Nicholl, a friend I knew from running around Mt. Rainier, and his friend Adrian Crane, an accomplished adventure racer from California, were both being helped by Joanne, a coworker of Ray's who, in shifts, crewed both runners from a van bearing the logo of a chicken/egg business. All were in good spirits; furthermore, if either Ray or Adrian had to stop, he'd join Joanne to help crew the other one.

But Jesse Riley needed help. A gangly dishwasher from Key West, Florida, Jesse had saved up money to ride a bus to Washington and had enlisted his friend, Tom, to crew him from a small rental car. Jesse had been walking eighteen hours a day and sleeping when he pleased, while Tom was grabbing bits of sleep in the car when he could. Both were wearing down, so we offered our motor home to help them.

Tom and I switched places for a while. He slept in our motor home while I drove his car into the night, crewing for Jesse. Jesse reached a checkpoint and stopped to get medical help for his swollen knee. The physician asked a few questions and concluded that Jesse was doing about all he could do, except stop walking. His knee was tightly wrapped, iced frequently, and constantly treated with anti-inflammatory drugs.

Jesse gave me instructions: drive ahead two miles, wait and see if I need you, then drive another two miles and repeat; every four miles, have my food ready. All his food was in the trunk of the car. When I opened the lid, all I saw were maple PowerBars.

He explained that he ate one PowerBar every four miles, a total of 125 bars for 500 miles. Other than that, he had gotten a meal in one town. And yesterday, when he passed a Safeway store, Tom had bought a loaf of white Wonder Bread that Jesse immediately wolfed down. His drinking needs were equally simple: water containing a squeeze of lemon.

Jesse eventually took a sleep break in our motor home, first icing his knee and then elevating his legs during rest. Soon Tom was refreshed enough to resume crewing. He also resumed calling the PowerBar company, trying to get them to sponsor Jesse.

By day eight, only two solo runners—Adrian and Jesse—had a chance to finish on time. An injured knee had forced Ray to stop after 380 miles, after which he helped crew for Adrian, who was following the relay schedule and completing the specified stage each day. Jesse was doing the go-as-you-please version He was behind Adrian but had a good chance to finish on time, too.

We drove to the finish line, where a thousand runners from relay teams were celebrating. I went to a booth to collect my T-shirt. When the clerk learned I had stopped after 260 miles, she explained that I didn't get one. When I protested that relay runners each received one for running a total of about 62 miles, and she explained that she was just following the rules, I realized this wasn't my finest moment.

We gathered in a large stadium for the awards presentation. Notable finishers included Fred and the Hat Man (so named because he wore a different hat each day), a two-person relay team, and the Ancient Flying Kiwis from New Zealand whose ten members, most in their 50s, were now warmed up to run the Boston Marathon the following week.

Adrian Crane, the only solo runner in the fixed-stage division to finish on time, received his award to thunderous applause. During the ceremonies, Jesse Riley, the only finisher in the go-as-you-please division, strode into the stadium and received his award to equally loud applause.

The best words about the race came three months later from Jesse, in his letter to *UltraRunning* magazine:

What I learned... is that when you're cold and hungry, tired and footsore, when you've been blinded all night long by the high beams of an endless succession of passing cars along narrow highways, when you can't keep anything down that you eat, but can't live without eating, when you're too weary to keep going, but in too much pain to sleep, when climbing the hills has sapped your energy and descending them has shredded your kneecaps, when it's been hours since you've seen anyone but your handler and days since you've seen your fellow competitors, when you've had every injury that can fit onto one overmatched body and everything possible has gone wrong, there's still a mind that knows it's not enough, two legs that can take at least one more step, an ideal worth fighting for, a dream worth any sacrifice to make a reality.

But wait; there's more. I was officially a DNF, which means "Did Not Finish." People who put smiley faces on everything will tell you it also means "Did Nothing Fatal," but I wasn't buying it. For five years, the disappointment of failing to finish the Lewis and Clark Trail Run stuck in my craw. Finally, I decided it was better late than never. I still had the course description for the final 240 miles. I could do that in two weekends.

I liked the way Bobby Wise had done the run, completely on his own. Maybe I could channel my early years, when I aspired to be a hobo, traveling around and taking life as it came. Indeed, I remembered fondly the time my brother, John, and I hitchhiked a few days and spent a night in Duluth, Minnesota wondering where to sleep. We didn't find a junk yard to provide suitable back seats we could use, so we settled for climbing into an empty boxcar in the railroad yards downtown, wondering where we'd wake up the next morning.

I knew that being a hobo wasn't as romantic as it's cracked up to be, but the lure of heading out on the road, free and independent, was irresistible. So on a Friday afternoon, I boarded a Greyhound bus going from Ellensburg to Biggs, Oregon. I got off, put on my pack, crossed the bridge over the Columbia River back into Washington, and said hello and good-bye to Maryhill State Park, where I had dropped out of the race five years ago.

A steep climb led to Highway 14, which wended west along the Columbia River all the way to Vancouver, Washington, 120 miles away and my destination for Sunday night. After a few hours, it was getting too dark to keep running. To the left, down by the river, I spotted Horsethief Lake State Park, where I had planned to spend the night. The place was visited by Lewis and Clark in 1805, though the lake itself was created later by the Dalles Dam, just downstream.

But the park was so far down below the road that going there and coming back up in the morning would add several tough, extra miles to my trip. So I just kept running until the highway crested a point overlooking the massively lit Dalles Dam. I walked fifty yards off the road and ducked into an orchard to sleep, hoping to leave early the next day without being seen.

The wind gusted as I blew up the $5 air mattress I had bought three days earlier at a local hardware store. I lay on it, wrapped only in a small, thin aluminized space blanket I had received at some race. The wind cut through the trees as I shivered through an uncomfortable night.

The next morning I slipped out of the orchard and resumed running west, stopping to eat a hearty breakfast in the small town of Lyle, where locals stared at the disheveled stranger in their midst. The day turned hot as I continued jogging the left side of the paved road, staring down at the Columbia River as cars whizzed past.

Temperatures reached into the 90s as I passed a road crossing over to Hood River, Oregon, a windsurfing mecca. The Columbia River was teeming with windsurfers. A complete wet suit, in good condition, lay on the road, perhaps blown off someone's van.

Saturday night I reached Beacon Rock State Park, put money in an envelope to pay for my campsite, and spent another cold, uncomfortable night, this time sleeping on my air mattress on top of a picnic table. The park was all mine.

Sunday brought pressure to make good time. I had to reach the Clark County Fairgrounds, just outside Vancouver, by 6 p.m. in order to get a ride from my friends Mark Bodamer and his girlfriend, Amber, who were flying into nearby Portland and then driving back to Ellensburg.

The temperature again sizzled into the 90s. Getting low on drink, I read in the old race manual that I'd soon reach a convenience store. When I arrived, all I found was a sign by the railroad tracks. *Things change in five years.* I continued on, thirsty.

The road curved through several tunnels, with separate train tunnels on the left. During the long-ago race, police officers had halted traffic when runners ran though. But today no one was here. I couldn't see through the tunnels because of their bends, and I saw very little room to flatten against the wall if vehicles, especially logging trucks, charged through. So I looked back until I saw no traffic, listened ahead for silence, gulped, and then ran through as fast as possible. Fear is a powerful motivator.

Camas, the paper mill town where Ray Nicholl's sore knee forced him to stop five years ago, offered a smoky welcome that irritated my nostrils and lungs. *How do people here put up with it?* I continued west on Highway 14. Tired and bored, I sampled roadside literature, finding publications that would never be allowed in my house and reading about options I never knew existed.

I reached Ft. Vancouver, a major hub of fur trading for the Hudson's Bay Company in the early 1800s. When fur trading declined, the U.S. Army took over and used it during the Civil War and World Wars I and II, after which the fort was restored and designated a National Historic Site.

Near Officer's Row, where 21 stately Victorian mansions graced a fine boulevard, I searched in vain for a road listed in the race manual. After running around, looking at street signs and asking local people, I finally found the road the unfound road was supposed to lead to. I shrugged and continued west until I reached the outskirts of Vancouver.

There a genetically blessed woman jogged my way. We briefly made eye contact, said "Hello," and continued on our separate ways. Fifteen minutes later, she had turned around and caught up to me, now going my direction. She was curious about what I was doing. When I explained, she asked if I needed a break; we'd go by her house in a few minutes, and I'd be welcome to stop by and have a shower and refreshments.

The possibilities, fueled by my recent roadside literature search, were intriguing. I could see it: a mysterious stranger arrives in town, seemingly out of nowhere. He comes into her life and magic happens for a short, sweet time. I could even picture the book title: *The Tunnels of Skamania County*.

Reality returned. I was happily married and had a great family; in addition, I was on a tight schedule if I was going to get a ride home tonight. I thanked her for her kind offer, and she turned for home. Twenty minutes later, she was wearing a short skirt and low-cut blouse and pulled alongside me in a shiny red convertible. She stopped and offered me a chilled bottle of Gatorade, which I gladly accepted, and then said "Good-bye," this time for good.

I reached the Clark County Fairgrounds with thirty minutes to spare, thoroughly drained by the heat. I stumbled into a pizza place, ordered, and telephoned Mark and Amber, who had just arrived in Portland after running the Vermont 100-Mile race. They were excited because Amber had just completed her first 100-miler while Mark had just completed the second leg of the Grand Slam—four specific 100-mile runs in one summer.

When they picked me up Mark asked, with a little hesitation, about all the new lines crisscrossing my forehead. I finally figured it out: while waiting for my pizza, I had crawled under the table and pressed my overheated head straight against the vent grating to enjoy the full blast of air conditioning.

One week-end down; one to go.

The next Friday, my running friend, Steve Varga—the same person who wrestled me in the parking lot by the Wonderland Trail—decided to drive along while I ran the final 120 miles of the Lewis and Clark course. He wanted to visit where he grew up and be part of the adventure. I wouldn't be much of a hobo now, but I'd get to camp properly and run with a lighter pack.

Near dusk, he dropped me off at the Clark County Fairgrounds near Vancouver. I ran fifteen miles, and then he picked me up in the dark and drove to a facility caring for his grandmother in her last days. We talked with her and fellow residents before setting up our tents on the lawn to sleep through a rainy night.

Saturday morning Steve drove me to where I had finished running the night before. I left on foot, enjoying a lighter pack than I had carried the week before, while he drove back to spend more time with his grandmother. My route wound north, passing through the lumber mill towns of Kelso and Longview, and then angled west on Highway 4, aiming for the Pacific Ocean. Early afternoon, Steve drove up and we stopped for food. Then he drove ahead to find us a place to camp.

Two hours later, I and a long line of cars were stopped at a road construction zone. I persuaded the flagger to wave me through with the promise that I'd be careful. That evening, when I found Steve at a campground along the Columbia River, the clerk said she'd been waiting for me. *Huh?* She explained that her husband was with the State Highway Patrol, and all day they had been monitoring some vagrant carrying a pack running west.

We camped by the river. Horns and shadowy shapes from ocean-going vessels shrouded in fog passed by our tiny tents all night long.

Near dawn on Sunday, I started running west on Highway 4 on what would be an uneventful, 50-mile day. Except for one thing: it was the final day. Time passed agreeably; I was tired, but excited about finishing.

Late afternoon, I climbed the final few hills leading into Fort

Canby State Park, near the small town of Ilwaco. I recognized where the huge, white "Finish" banner had been strung five years earlier. This place, then swarming with celebrating runners and crews, now welcomed only Steve and me.

It was enough. We walked across the beach to where the Columbia River met the Pacific Ocean. Finally, finally, the cool waters off Cape Disappointment washed away my own, five-year-old disappointment.

Over a fine seafood dinner, I could only smile when Steve claimed I was disqualified because of that ½ mile or so in Ft. Vancouver where I couldn't find the right road. And I laughed when he reminded me that I still didn't have the T-shirt.

Then we did the math. Since it took a little over five years to complete 500 miles, my average pace, perhaps a record, was about ¼ mile per day. Which reminded me of Steven Wright's words: "everywhere is within walking [or running] distance—if you have the time."

7 HARDROCK

By 1996, I had finished more than a dozen 100-mile runs on trails and tracks. In my 50s, I decided it was now or never to take on Hardrock, the hardest 100-mile trail run in the United States.

What makes Hardrock so tough? The course gains a total of 33,000 feet, more (its organizers gladly point out) than going from sea level to the summit of Mount Everest. The total descent is the same. The average grade is 12%. Keep in mind that highways with 6% downhill grades have runaway ramps for trucks. In addition, the *average* elevation is near timberline, a little above 11,000 feet, and the highest point is 14,048-foot Handies Peak.

The course is one loop in the scenic, rugged San Juan Mountains of southwestern Colorado beginning and ending in 9300-foot Silverton. The two other towns en route are 7700-foot Ouray and 8700-foot Telluride, where we come *down* for air from the high country. Each year the course reverses direction from the previous year.

Because it is so difficult, Hardrock has a time limit of 48 hours, 12 hours longer than any other 100-miler in the country.

Over the years, two amazing performances stand out. Of more than two thousand runners since 1992, only one—23-year-old Kyle Skaggs from New Mexico—finished in less than 24 hours. The other, John DeWalt from Pennsylvania, finished the race thirteen consecutive times *starting at*—are you ready for this?— age 60.

The folks who designed the course and entrance requirements were mostly scientists who worked at nearby Los Alamos National Laboratory, home of the Manhattan Project that developed the atomic bombs dropped on Japan to end World War II. People allowed to run Hardrock were chosen by a complicated system fully understood only by, well, rocket scientists.

When I was selected to run Hardrock, I was both elated and wondering whether I was biting off more than I could chew. One thing was clear: my only chance of finishing this beautiful beast was to arrive early to acclimatize and learn the course.

Fortunately, runners were allowed to accompany those marking the course two weeks before the race began. Better yet, Charlie Thorn (a scientist at Los Alamos), the head course marker, kindly invited several of us to stay at his house during our time in Silverton.

Several days before Charlie arrived from Los Alamos to open up his house, I stopped at Montrose, Colorado to look up John and Ginny. Several months earlier we had met at a run in

Portland, Oregon. When I had mentioned I was going to run
Hardrock, they said they lived nearby, had always wanted to see
some of the course, and wondered if I would like them to pace me
there. Now they said they still wanted to pace me and invited me
in to stay the night. We made plans to meet in Telluride (where
pacing could begin during the race) in two-plus weeks.

Sixty miles from Melrose was Silverton, race headquarters.
Once in town, I spotted a man wearing a Hardrock T-shirt. I
rushed up to him and, a little breathlessly, asked about the race
and whether he'd done it. When he looked puzzled, I saw his shirt
was about the Hardrock Café. I shuffled away, desperately trying
to become invisible.

Silverton, covered in snow much of the winter and spring and
vulnerable to avalanches, springs to life in the summer. The big
event each day is the train arriving from Durango, disgorging its
passengers to shop for several hours in town, and then taking
them back. As I munched a funnel cake on Main Street,
surrounded by tourists that had just arrived for the day, the
proprietor explained that many shop owners here were seasonal,
operating here in the summer and in warmer places during the
winter.

With time on my hands, I explored Ouray and Telluride. At
the edge of Ouray was a fine complex of outdoor hot springs
where I lazed under the stars, talking with locals and sipping

coffee, before retiring to sleep in my aging Subaru station wagon parked inconspicuously (I hoped) on the street.

Telluride was more glamorous. I ambled around, listening to locals talk about celebrities who had homes nearby such as Oprah (thumbs up), Sylvester Stallone (thumbs down), and Christie Brinkley (mixed thumbs). Down by the park, a bluegrass festival was in full swing with counterculture folks basking in the sun and their VW vans, painted with flowers, lounging in the parking lot.

The next morning, after another night sleeping on the street, it was time to check out part of the course. I puffed up a steep trail we'd be descending during the race and stopped for a minute to catch my breath. Julie, a fit, fifty-something hiker walked by, introduced herself, and asked about my running pack. I explained I was here to run Hardrock and was checking out the course. Intrigued, she invited me to dinner.

That afternoon, when I had finished my trail expedition, I wandered around through Telluride before spotting a van carrying Schwann Frozen Foods. I asked the driver to give me the best dessert he could for the $8 I was carrying, and walked away with a strawberry pie to bring to dinner. Julie and her husband, Frank, graciously welcomed me, gave me a shower, a fine dinner and conversation, and a bunk bed. They promised to meet me during the race in a couple of weeks when I ran through Telluride.

The next day Charlie Thorn arrived in Silverton, so I made

myself at home there and joined a crew of runners to go with him each day to mark a dozen or so miles of the course. One day he drove us over the worst road I've ever seen. Sitting in the open bed of a pickup truck with other bouncing crew members, we lurched from rock to rock while staring at a precipitous drop-off. One turn was so tight that Charlie had to stop and back up. The rear end of his truck stuck out into space and I wasn't the only one closing my eyes.

Every day, for a week, we spent six or so hours traveling to and marking a small part of the course. Each evening I thought: *how can I possibly run this section, plus the other ones I've seen, plus all the others I haven't seen, back-to-back-to-back during the race?*

We returned to Silverton each afternoon so tired that I thought about the story an older friend told me. When he had finished a solo run around Mt. Hood, about 42 miles, my friend was completely spent. He lay down on a bench near Timberline Lodge, exhausted, disheveled, eyes closed, and with one arm drooping down. A man passing by pressed a $10 bill into his hand and said: "Here, buddy. Here's something for a meal."

The Hardrock course was epic, intimidating and literally left you breathless. Entering and leaving the three towns, our route took us through forests. Much of the rest was above timberline, a mixture of meadows, boulder fields, and peaks. Patches of snow dotted especially the north faces where, on race day, ropes would be set in the most dangerous places. Some trails followed ledges with steep drop-offs. The views on top were stunning and sometimes extended for fifty miles.

One week before the race our work was done; it was time to rest and get strong. More runners arrived. One was Joel Zucker, who was staying at Charlie's house. Joel was a 5-foot-3-inch, 42-year-old, outspoken, dog-loving librarian from New York who had high blood pressure and who cofounded the most widely used email discussion group for ultrarunners. He had run Hardrock the previous year, finishing shortly after the 48-hour cutoff time. He was determined to become an official finisher this year.

The night before the race my good friend, Mark Bodamer, arrived and slept at Charlie's house. Mark had won the Mohican 100-Mile Run in Ohio and was the first person I knew personally to do the Grand Slam—finishing four specific 100-mile runs in one summer. He was an outstanding runner but had had little time to train, and none of it at high altitude.

Race day arrived. Ninety-two of us tried to stay warm in the chilly mountain air until we were released at six a.m. to start running, this year in the counterclockwise direction. I felt exceptionally strong and well prepared. After climbing a steep trail and slogging through a creek we reached the nine-mile checkpoint. A few miles later, still feeling strong, I charged up another hill, looking back to see if anyone was catching me. Seeing no one, I keep pushing, knowing I was really putting distance on the next runner.

After 25 minutes, still seeing no one behind me, or ahead of me, and having not seen a trail marker for a while, I began to wonder if I was on course. Soon I met people on horseback coming my way. They told me I had missed a turn.

I reversed directions, ran all the way back to where I had made the mistake, and got back on course, going from eighth to last place. It would be a sign of things to come; before my journey was finished, I would get lost four times, often on sections (like this one) I had helped mark. The lost time and, maybe more important, lost energy would cost me dearly. I had hoped to finish high in the pack; now my only goal was to finish.

Back on course, I said the Serenity Prayer and started catching up to other runners, enjoying their company. To my surprise, and disappointment, I eventually caught up to Mark, who was struggling in the thin air. We spent some good time together, wished each other well, and I moved ahead.

The day brought many stream crossings, stunning views above timberline, and meadows adorned with columbine, paintbrush, asters, irises, delphinium and other wildflowers. Each ascent and descent took a piece of me, as did my occasional wanderings off-course. Runners were far apart by now, and I went hours without seeing anyone.

Near the top of one peak, I was pelted by hail and lit up by lightning. A few miles from there a hiker had been killed by lightning a year ago, and we all knew that a peak was a bad place to be in this kind of storm. *Should I retreat and wait out the squall, or continue to the top and hustle down the other side to get out of danger? Duh. It's a race.*

Late afternoon, after 38 miles, the trail skirted patches of snow and snaked up to Handies Peak, one of Colorado's many 14-ers (14,000-foot peaks). On top of the highest place I'd ever been on foot was a 360-degree view of majestic proportions where I could see my trail for miles angling down to the Grouse Gulch aid station. I arrived there at dusk and pulled out my flashlight for the coming night.

An endless climb in the cooling dark took me over Engineer Pass, and then to a 4300-foot descent. Early on the way down I slipped into a creek and fell in up to my shoulders. I scrambled out and started running, now to restore my body heat.

The descent continued through a section whose sharp drop-offs along the trail had spooked me when I had run it in daylight before the race. Near the bottom, past the drop-off, I fell backwards down a bank and crashed into a tree. In pain and shock I called out for help. Blood was running down my forehead, I was sure my wrist was broken, and my run was over. But it was

1:30 a.m., and nobody else was around. Five minutes later, I retrieved my flashlight, still on, and resumed running.

I reached the Uncompaghre River, just upstream from a dam, grabbed the rope, set for this race, and waded across. A few miles later, I reached civilization, the 57-mile checkpoint at Ouray, and tried to regroup in the dark.

What comes down must go up. The 4400-foot climb out of Ouray, the longest of the race, brought another creek crossing. Having had my feet in water too much of the time, and feeling blisters with every step, I tried to stay dry by crossing on a wet, downhill-slanting log. Half way across I slipped, plunging into the creek, but at least landed on my feet.

Wet and sore, I neared Virginius Pass as day two dawned. I crawled the steep ascent on patches of scree and snow. *Ten steps, catch your breath, do it again, and try not to slip back down.* On top was an aid station, where I thanked and saluted the wonderful volunteers who had portered in all the supplies and were staying there for many hours to help us.

The route then seemed to descend right back to where I had begun the final ascent to this Pass. *What's going on? Why did the course designers make us do that final climb? For their amusement? Am I just a monkey they're jerking around? If they're going to treat us like that, there's no way I'm not going to finish this thing.*

An endless descent led into Telluride, our final oasis, 28 miles from the finish line. True to their promise, Frank and Julie met and greeted me. They had brought chocolate ice cream, which I gladly wolfed down. I bade them farewell and thanked them for all their kindness.

I left with Ginny, my first pacer, and was very happy to have her company. For the last twelve hours I had been completely alone except for brief stops at aid stations. Our ascent out of Telluride was long and tiring, but Ginny loved the beauty surrounding us and helped me appreciate it, too. Her energy helped mine. Easy conversation took my mind off my discomfort. I relaxed mentally and trusted her to find the trail markers.

After several good hours, I gratefully bid Ginny good-bye and welcomed John as my new pacer. Soon we approached Grant-Swamp Pass, a place I was worried about. When I had been there before the race, marking the course and going in the other direction, our marking crew had paused on top. I had looked over the edge where we then were going down (and now had to climb up) and thought there was no way to get down a slope that steep. That day a Hawaiian runner, who had finished smoking a funny cigarette on top, just plunged down into the scree and snow, sort of glissading in places and keeping his legs moving as best he could to stay upright. When the rest of us saw him down below, still alive, we gulped and followed suit.

But now we had to go up that wall. We found a climbing line used by the runners ahead of us and proceeded on all fours, gasping for breath and lying against the hill to keep from slipping down. *Crawl up a few steps. Claw onto anything you can. Catch your breath. Repeat.* Somehow, eventually, we made it. Once safely on top, John revealed, with great relief, that he feared heights and couldn't have done that ascent two years earlier.

The remaining miles took forever. I could do little but walk as the temperature neared freezing and a headwind chilled us. Into my second night without sleep, exhausted on a moonless night, I experienced tunnel vision as I peered vacantly through the narrow beam from my flashlight, looking for reflective trail markers.

Things just don't look right. Before the race I had run this section twice, but in daylight, and now I knew we were off course. I tried to explain that to John, who kept saying we were okay. I wandered down side paths, trying to find a marker, but John kept calling me back.

The trees and bushes are attacking me. Those white, wispy figures are trying to kill me. I yelled and swung my arms to ward them off. They flitted away, mocking me, and attacked again. In the middle of our battle, Hal Winton and his pacer suddenly appeared, said "Hello," and jogged past.

Hal Winton? I had met Hal years ago when I had run the Angeles Crest 100-Mile Race, which he helped direct for many years. I saw him again when he joined our trail-marking crew before this race. Hal, 64 years old, had been camping in his motor home all summer near Silverton, preparing for this race.

God bless you, Hal, for showing me we're on course after all. I'm proud to finish behind you, and congratulations on your great run. And thank you, John, for keeping me on course and putting up with me.

John and I waded across Mineral Creek and lumbered the final two, paved miles into Silverton. Up ahead, I heard the reception for Hal as he finished a little after midnight. A few minutes later, it was my turn to feel the joy and relief of reaching the Kendall Mountain Ski Hut. *It's over. I did it.*

I thanked Ginny and John for all their great help and bade them a very fond farewell. I celebrated with Mark, who'd had to stop about half-way, unable to overcome not training at altitude. Yet he had kindly come to the finish line in the middle of the night to welcome me and give me a ride to Charlie's house to shower and catch a few hours of sleep.

The next morning we gathered for breakfast and the awards ceremony. We forty-two finishers each received a numbered print of a painting of Buffalo Boy Tram Shed commissioned for this race. I could only smile and shake my head; it was a picture of the place I had reached right after getting lost the first time.

Back at Charlie's house, I talked with Joel Zucker. With

contagious joy he told me about his dramatic race to beat the 48-hour clock. After a night struggling with demons and course markers, he had found the legs and strength to run the final three miles as hard as he could, laughing and crying at the same time as he crossed the finish line with ten minutes to spare.

The next year, Joel would return and finish in the same time. And the following year, he would have yet another close call with the clock, this time beating the 48-hour time limit by 22 minutes. But 36 hours later, when he and his pacer were driving to an airport to catch their flight home, Joel suddenly suffered a brain aneurism. Rushed to a hospital, he never regained consciousness.

Joel loved Hardrock, and the feeling was mutual. After his death, race organizers established the Joel Zucker Memorial Scholarship, given annually to Silverton High School or surrounding area seniors who contributed substantially to the run and were going to college. A memorial plaque to Joel now rests atop Grant-Swamp Pass.

Rest in peace, my friend.

8 GREAT DIVIDE RIDE I

One-hundred mile trail runs were, for me, the gold standard. Completing them in as fast a time as possible took an all-out effort. After running Hardrock, I still wanted to do new 100s, which were popping up everywhere. But things weren't quite the same. I still enjoyed the challenge, and the new places to see, but I had already finished the hardest one and, probably, the most beautiful.

Three runs, none of them 100 miles, remained on my all-time to-do list: Boston Marathon, Comrades (53 or so miles in South Africa), and across the Grand Canyon and back. For me, none of those would be races; I just wanted to run and enjoy them. Little did I know, however, that late in my 50s I was about to reach a turning point, and my to-do list would expand to include a whole new type of adventure.

In my day job as a chemistry professor, I met lots of interesting people. One day, I was socializing with Barney Erickson, my Dean, and he was shaking his head, muttering about the trip he didn't get to take. He had planned to lead Explorer scouts from his church on a two-week mountain bike ride in northern Montana, but it was cancelled at the last minute.

They were going to pedal the first 500 miles of a course newly mapped by Adventure Cycling, a company in Missoula, Montana. The full 2500-mile route, called the Great Divide Ride, is the longest off-pavement bicycle route in the world, and winds from the Canadian border to the Mexican border. It snakes along the Continental Divide, crossing that ridge 27 times.

As I listened to Barney, something deep inside suddenly bubbled to the surface as I heard myself say, "I'll go with you next summer."

Where did that come from? Part of it came from knowing, after nearly two decades of running long distances, that I was fit enough. *I should be able to keep up with Barney.* Another part came from me, without realizing it, being ready for something new. Barney's timing was perfect.

Like most runners, I occasionally rode a bicycle. Triathletes, of course, make biking a regular part of their training, along with running and swimming. And I knew a few ultrarunners who also competed in long-distance bicycle races. But neither situation applied to me.

I'd never ridden a bicycle more than 25 miles, and I hadn't ridden one outdoors more than forty times in the last forty years.

Like many runners I'd occasionally cycle, both indoors and outside, as a form of cross-training. When I'd had running injuries, for example, I occasionally rode a bicycle to maintain fitness while letting the injury heal. And the first time I gained entry into the Western States 100-mile race, I had cycled early in the morning as an extra, low-impact workout for the day.

But that was it. Two bicycles were collecting spider webs in our storage shed. Our daughter, Lindsay, had one; the other arrived when a friend of our son, Jedd, left a rusty three-speed bike at our house and didn't want it back. We had tried to sell it for $5 at a yard sale, but nobody would take it. It had just two working gears, the most I'd ever used, and it was my outdoor bicycle.

So why do I suddenly want to go on this mountain bike trip with Barney? As I thought about it, the answer became clear. What I love about ultrarunning—the challenge of getting in shape and heading out into the unknown in interesting and often beautiful places, the adventure of taking things as they come and solving problems as they arise—also applied to this bicycle trip. I could become a gentleman hobo.

Barney explained that the Great Divide Ride was 70% on unpaved county, logging and forest service roads, 20% on jeep and two-track roads, 5% on single-track trails, and 5% on pavement. We'd carry our camping gear and pass through enough towns that we'd never have to carry more than a three-day food supply. And I'd get to gobble whatever I wanted—even junk food that too rarely inhabited my (Laurae's) kitchen at home.

I bought the map and read about the course. A minimum of three riders was recommended for safety, so I recruited Mel van Houten, a local ultrarunning friend, to join the party. You first met Mel, in this book, throwing up near his tent after completing a tough climb at the end of day one going around Mt. Rainier on the Wonderland Trail.

A few years earlier he and his wife, Keiko, had driven through town on their way to check out a retirement place on the coast. They had stopped in Ellensburg (where they had never been before) for the night and grabbed a bite to eat, a motel room and a circular listing local properties for sale. They lingered the next day, liked the area and the prices, bought a house and retired here.

Mel was the oldest, most experienced, and fastest biker of our trio, but Barney was no slouch. I knew they would be fine. But I knew almost nothing about bicycling and wasn't sure whether a year to prepare could bring me up to speed. Since the route was mostly on dirt, I bought a used mountain bike, learned a little about it, and started riding in earnest to get my legs, neck, back and butt in shape.

I didn't—couldn't—know that when I told Barney I'd go biking with him that a whole new world would open up to me, one that could continue even after my running days were over.

Our plunge into the unknown began in late July when Mel, Barney and I piled into Barney's pickup truck and drove to Eureka, Montana. After setting up our tents that evening, we figured out how best to cycle the ten miles between there and the Canadian border at Roosville, where the Great Divide Ride officially begins. We decided that Mel and Barney would drive north to the border with their bicycles while I would bike there and meet them. Then we'd switch places; I'd load my bike into Barney's truck and drive back to Eureka while Mel and Barney pedaled back.

We met at Roosville as planned. All went well until we snapped some photos just south of the entrance into Canada and started walking back to our bicycles. A siren blared and a U.S. border guard on the other side of the road crooked his finger at us. He barked out that we had walked over the (invisible and unmarked) border into Canada when we took the photos; now we had to pass through U.S. Customs before we could return to our bikes. *What can you do?* After a testy few minutes, he dismissed us, forgetting to say, "Have a nice day."

The next morning, we broke camp and loaded thirty or so pounds of clothing, food, water, tents, bicycle repair gear and cooking equipment onto our bicycles. Barney towed his gear in a trailer while Mel and I crammed ours into panniers (saddle bags) attached to our rear racks (that is, our *bicycles'* rear racks). On our way out of town, we stopped at a hardware store to buy pepper spray to protect against bears, especially grizzlies. The clerk just smiled and said a group of bikers earlier in the week had cleaned out his stock. We rode away, excited and unprotected. *We're really going to do this.*

As we pedaled south, we talked. I knew Mel because we both ran long distances, and I'd known Barney a long time because we worked at the same university. But the first time Barney and Mel had met was yesterday, when we stepped into Barney's truck to drive to Eureka.

Barney and Mel were an odd couple in several ways. Mel was a leathery, lanky man whose pounds were stretched taut across his 6-foot-5-inch frame. He towered over Barney and me, both sub-6-feet. If Mel was a string bean, Barney and I were butter beans. Barney had close-cropped hair and a cheerful face that looked a bit like a grown-up cherub.

They differed in other ways, too. A mathematics professor, Barney knew numbers, planned meticulously and was both a nice and no-nonsense guy. Mel was laid back, took things as they came, and cared more about words (he spoke six languages) than numbers.

Mel was a Michigan native who long ago had shed his Dutch

Orthodox roots. Barney was a Utah native who held firmly to his Mormon faith and had served several years as lay leader (bishop) of his local church. While entirely respectful of each other, we soon concluded that religion wasn't a fruitful topic for discussion.

Politics was a different matter. Barney, as you might expect, was a conservative, straight-arrow guy with traditional values. Mel was liberal, his views molded by his lifetime as a financial officer in U.S. embassies around the world. As we pedaled down the road we worked on solving the world's problems.

After ten miles, pavement gave way to dirt and nonexistent traffic as we meandered east, squinting into the rising sun, heading toward the Rocky Mountains and the Continental Divide. Soon Mel and I had to repair flat tires. We climbed 2500 feet up the Whitefish Divide, with Barney feeling the extra work towing his trailer. Once on top, we shot down through wild, tall-timber country, keeping our eyes pealed for bears, and skirted the Flathead River for several miles.

By 6:30 p.m., we'd ridden 53 miles and entered Flathead National Forest. Since you can camp most anywhere on Forest Service and BLM (Bureau of Land Management) lands, we spotted a buggy little spot by a creek and put up our tents. Not another soul was in sight as we prepared to cook our first camp supper. The line from Barney's fuel canister leaked and caught on fire. While he tried to put it out, Mel and I scratched our heads, both to ward off mosquitoes and to figure out how to use our cooking systems. *Maybe we should have practiced this ahead of time.* Eventually we downed truly dreadful meals, hoisted a bear bag and dropped off to sleep.

The morning greeted us as we rode ten miles up to Red Meadow Lake, passing by bear scat so fresh we could smell it and see its steam rising into the cool, crisp air. On a long, steep downhill we met three young riders who had started the Great Divide Ride earlier that summer at the Mexican border. We stopped to talk. They told us that New Mexico was the toughest section, with rough terrain and zillions of goat heads (thorns) that puncture tire tubes. What works best, they said, was using inner tubes coated with Slime, gooey green ooze that fills and seals small punctures.

Today I hurt where, shall we say, the body meets the saddle. In training I had ridden many rough miles, helping my rear end and saddle break each other in. For now, though, the saddle was winning. Constantly bumpy roads were literally a pain in the butt. *Thank goodness I brought along Bag Balm.*

Mel, our strongest rider, was the only one who didn't bother to carry a map. Mr. Laid Back occasionally looked at one of ours and then rode ahead, stopping a few miles down the road and waiting for us while reading the next few pages of his paperback. Barney and I would cross our fingers each time he disappeared, hoping he'd stay on course.

The day's 40-mile ride took us past Whitefish Lake and into the pretty town of Whitefish. We arrived in early afternoon and took an overpriced campsite. After a shower and steak dinner (spared, at least for the night, from eating our own cooking), we fell asleep to the gentle pita pat of rain on our tents.

The next morning we pedaled ten mellow miles into Columbia Falls. When Mel stopped for a latte, I waited astride my bicycle, my right foot on the curb. As cars moseyed past, I lost my balance and started falling sideways. My left foot, still attached to the pedal, couldn't escape. Time froze as I clunked onto the pavement, lay in the street, and tried to look composed as passing motorists observed a guy who thought he was going to ride the Great Divide.

After 28 more gentle miles we passed Swan Lake and angled two miles off course on a pot-holed road into Bigfork, a lovely little town that has a pretty campground where the Swan River empties into Flathead Lake. After dinner, we retired to our campground where I, armed with ignorance, fiddled with my bicycle to make its gears shift more smoothly. My ideas didn't work, so Barney and Mel chimed in with theirs. Three cooks put my bike in the soup. By the time we all finished fixing my bicycle, its twenty-four working gears had dwindled to two.

Now what do we do? I can't ride on like this. My trip is over if

I can't get this bike repaired, and it is many, many miles to the nearest bicycle shop. No one at this campground (certainly including us) knows what to do.

Then I remembered seeing a group of bicycles lying in a grassy area in town when we had eaten dinner. We rode back there and discovered a bike tour passing through town. The tour group had a mechanic who kindly diagnosed and fixed the problem: a shifter cable so twisted and tortured by all of our "adjustments" that it had to be replaced.

Phew. I will get to ride tomorrow after all, and none of us is going to "fix" my bike again.

We awakened to the first of four straight days of record heat. We puffed five miles and 2000 feet up to the summit of Crane Mountain, cruised a few miles along the top, and wound down through old growth larch, Douglas fir and white pine. The exhilarating descent took us past the town of Swan Lake and the Swan Lake National Wildlife Refuge. The woods and sparkling waters reminded us we were in "A River Runs through It" country.

Barney was in his element. A lifelong hunter and fisherman, he had developed a keen eye for wildlife and regaled us with his outdoors adventures—his summer jobs in Utah and nearby states where he had done trail and other work and had survived some close calls with human and other animals.

Then our conversation turned to bicycling. Barney told about his 1500-mile bike trip to Yellowstone National Park and back with a visiting professor from Japan who nearly expired in the heat. Mel chimed in with his biking stories—winning not only his 50s age group but also the 40s age group in a bicycle race in Japan and riding in such diverse places as Cambodia, Patagonia, South Africa, Ecuador, Poland and Vietnam. When it came to biking stories, I had nothing to offer.

After nine hours of fun in too much sun, we dragged our carcasses into a spot on the map called Cedar Creek Campground. The place was all ours as we skinny-dipped and washed away layers of grime. Our meals were slightly less dreadful. *We're learning, however slowly.* Sleep came quickly.

We awakened, hardly fresh, and my bike greeted me with a flat tire. While I worked on repairs, Barney, the mathematician, studied the map. Our chief planner and organizer, he calculated that we should be able to camp tonight at Clearwater Lake, 47 miles down the dirt road.

We wilted on another hot day as we headed south, flanked by the Swan Mountain Range on our left (east) and the Mission Mountains on our right (west). We drank in beautiful scenery and, later, a Pepsi when Mel and I stopped at a rustic bar that appeared out of nowhere. We guzzled the cool liquid, laced with sugar and caffeine and carrying the signature delights of carbonated beverages: a fizz on the tongue and a slight tang due to carbonic acid forming from the dissolved carbon dioxide reacting with water.

The day was a grunt. Literally. Miles were hard-won as we climbed to 5000 feet. Barney walked his bicycle, and its flat tire, the final half mile down to Clearwater Lake. We camped alone in a pretty site that we were too tired to fully appreciate. But eating supper and watching the sun set as a deer came down to the water helped restore our spirits.

A short, 25-mile ride awaited us the next day. We needed it. We started pedaling at 7 a.m., as usual, up a steep, four-mile climb to 7000-foot Richmond Peak in the Bob Marshall Wilderness, home to many a grizzly bear. Downed trees, rocks and severe drop-offs along a slide zone put us on red alert. A fall would do serious damage, so we went slowly and welcomed the adventure.

Finally on top, we descended on a trail so overgrown with trees that in places we had to force our way through the branches, using our arms also to shield our faces from damage *How, in a few years, will any riders be able to get through?* But on that day our ride was challenging, bracing and fun.

We reached the trailhead of the Seeley Lake Nordic Ski Trails. A two-mile gravel road took us off the main route and into Seeley Lake, where Mel had a friend who, with his wife, welcomed us to stay in their fine log home. My saddle sores were especially grateful. We enjoyed showers and good conversation over a steak dinner while staring outside the front window at a wildlife show starring a large elk. For dessert, we slept on soft beds.

With thanks, we said good-bye in the morning and pedaled into Seeley Lake to eat breakfast while washing our clothes and studying our maps for the day's ride. After twenty-six miles, we exited Lolo National Forest and rode up to Trixi's Saloon near the small burg of Ovando. We sat outside munching burgers when a logger walked by, noticed our bikes, and asked what we were doing. We talked a while and Barney mentioned that we'd soon reach Lincoln, home of the Unabomber, Ted Kaczynski. The logger said he knew Ted and thought well of him. "Ted helped lots of local kids learn mathematics," he explained, "and his ideas about society were right. He just carried things a little too far."

We rode into the afternoon with a temperature once again topping 90 degrees. Late in the day, our energy and water supplies on E, we climbed two miles off course to camp at Coopers Lake. Mel and Barney filtered water using pumps that weren't working as well as when we started the trip. I had been using iodine solution, adding two capfuls to a quart of water and waiting thirty minutes for the chemicals to work. But I was tired of the iodine taste, so I tried using Barney's pump. Filling my three quart bottles took 1020 pumps. I counted every one.

I walked from the lake up to my tent with a sore right arm

and found the only other person in camp talking with Barney and Mel. He had kindly brought us pieces of elk steak to enjoy for supper. We went to bed early, knowing the next day would be tough.

It was. Our first climb was 1500 feet. Enjoying the cool morning, we had nearly reached the summit when my chain broke. *Now what do I do?* None of us had ever fixed a broken chain. The bicycle equipment bag under my saddle did carry a chain tool and a couple of replacement links, so eventually I figured out how to take out the broken link and replace it. *But now where exactly do I thread the chain when I put it back on my bicycle?* None of us knew. The obvious solution finally dawned on us: *all we have to do is look at one of the other bicycles.*

We pedaled into Lincoln, ate lunch, and headed south past the cabin where the Unabomber lived before he was hauled off to prison. A 2000-foot climb led to our first crossing of the Continental Divide at almost 7000 feet. Our map gave two options—the gnarly route, straight up with several stream crossings, or a longer, gentler ascent.

Mel biked and walked straight up while Barney and I chose the other way. Eventually we found each other on top. We cooled off on a descent through scenic Marsh Creek Canyon in the Helena National Forest. After a few miles we reached Grady Ranches, a pretty camping area by Marsh Creek, and had the place to ourselves.

Here I observed that Mel's culinary standards were higher than mine. I had already watched him in restaurants (which in Montana were sometimes a combination casino/café/bowling alley) ask the waiter if the mashed potatoes were "real" before ordering. Now, while his camp meal was cooking, he enjoyed hors d'oeuvres consisting of a small bottle of cabernet sauvignon and a tin of smoked mussels. I, in contrast, sipped iodine-treated water from Marsh Creek and munched on a Little Debbie donut.

Although the heat wave had ended, the morning brought us a challenging day (this is a recording) in which we would cross the Continental Divide twice. We ground our way up the first, passing clear cuts and old mines. Mel decided to take an alternate route for a few miles and got lost, while Barney got a flat tire to even out the timing. Eventually we all found each other.

This is as good a time as any to explain that when we went our separate ways, we were flying by the seat of our pants. Our only communication device (besides our voices) was Barney's cell phone, which almost never had service and was virtually useless. And because Mel didn't carry a map, he either borrowed one of ours (if Barney and I stayed together) or took a look at the map before riding off and remembered as best he could.

Our second crossing of the Divide was a bit lower, at 6000-foot Priest Pass. We crested and descended together as Barney got his second flat tire of the day. As usual, it was the rear tire, perhaps because of its extra stress from pulling a trailer.

After nine and a half hours, we limped into Helena, arriving just in time to find a bicycle shop open so we could buy more inner tubes and chain links. Originally a gold camp named Last Chance Gulch, this city became the state capitol in 1875, ousting Virginia City for the honor. We treated ourselves to a motel room and scrubbed away more layers of trail dirt.

The Adventure Cycling folks who devised and mapped our route know Montana well, and they showed it the next day by offering us some single-track trails south of Helena. A seven-mile climb up Grizzly Gulch, followed by eight miles down toward Park Lake, all on dirt roads, brought us to that option. From there we could ride five miles to Interstate 15 at Clancy and follow it and frontage roads into Basin, our destination for the night. Or we could ride 26 miles of rough jeep roads and single-track trails into Basin.

Barney opted for the roads while Mel and I chose the trails. Barney would reach Basin long before we did, so he'd find us a place to spend the night. We parted company.

Mel and I had one map between us, and it was mine, so I was the navigator, which is rarely a good idea. We waded through knee-deep water, lifting our bikes as best we could to keep our gear dry, pedaled across cattle guards, and headed up a steep four-wheel-drive track we couldn't ride in places. Our reward was miles of trails, used mostly by ATVs, that featured more rocks and roots than I could handle. Now in Beaverhead-Deerlodge National Forest, featuring Douglas fir, lodgepole pine, and other shade-giving trees, Mel and I often had to dismount, walk, and remount. But the temperature was cool, our energy was good, and our obstacle course took us through lovely meadows.

Eventually we reached the outskirts of Basin, barely eluding a trucker who welcomed us with half of the peace sign. Barney was waiting, rested and cheerful, at the Merry Widow Campground.

Always an early riser, Barney by now had hardened us to the routine: wake up at six; eat breakfast; pack up and start riding at seven. After ugly experiments early in our trip, I'd learned from Barney and Mel that two packets of instant oatmeal added to boiling water made a fast and adequate meal. Like Mel, I chased the oatmeal with a cup of coffee. Barney passed on coffee, honoring a Mormon practice of not drinking hot caffeinated beverages. But apparently cold caffeinated drinks were okay, because Barney drank Pepsi with gusto. *God works in mysterious ways.*

Eleven hours on the road the next day seemed easy. While we cycled past deserted mines, crossed wetlands, and rode through a tunnel, our conversation flowed as we discovered that we, like many men of our generation, shared a lifelong love of baseball. We pedaled on good gravel roads along Interstate 15, with Mel waxing rhapsodic about his beloved Detroit Tigers and Barney reliving glory days of his Boston Red Sox.

After thirteen miles, our conversation ended as we rode onto Interstate 15, making our fourth crossing of the Continental Divide and diving five miles down into Butte. The descent was thrilling and unnerving as vehicles blasted past and we tried to control our vibrating, heavily-loaded bicycles. Coasting at 35 miles per hour, I pictured a truck or RV smearing me across the pavement if I had a flat tire or any other mechanical failure.

Barney led the descent; the trailer that slowed him going uphill now propelling him down. Next came Mel, but I was gaining on him, getting close enough that our tires would soon touch. I was about to squeeze my brakes when he sensed my presence and gave me a lesson in aerodynamics. Without pedaling a stroke, he folded his lanky frame forward and down over his handlebars, instantly accelerating away from me.

We entered Butte, a rugged town and home to the World Museum of Mining on Hellroarin' Gulch. The city's huge, open-pit mine once provided much of the world's copper. We stopped briefly to resupply and then rode south as storm clouds gathered.

Our fifth crossing of the Continental Divide was above 7000 feet. No sign marked the spot on top where we sat and enjoyed the open, park-like vista featuring sage and aspen flanked by the distant Pioneer Mountains. We called it a day two miles later at a pretty, anonymous little campsite tucked along a stream.

The next morning, after riding ten miles on the northern flank of Mount Fleecer, we reached Interstate 15 and another decision point. Barney, apparently having better control of his testosterone, opted for the paved alternate route into Wise River, our destination for the night. Mel and I took the road less traveled, and soon found out why.

In places the terrain was unrideable for Mel and me. But we tried valiantly. Our bikes, bearing so much extra weight on their rear racks, were as unbalanced as their riders. I clenched my teeth and pedaled furiously up a climb so steep that the front wheel lifted off. Suddenly my steed and I executed a less-than-artistic backward somersault.

In addition to the usual layout, our map carried written directions keyed to the tenth of a mile. But our cyclometers (now called computers) often varied by a few tenths from the numbers on the map, so we took those instructions with a few grains of salt. That day we reached the point where we were riding on a faint track looking for a right turn "cutting through a grassy meadow and aimed at a solitary fence" off in the distance.

While continuing to look, our path took Mel and me down, and down. It didn't seem like we should be doing this, so we kept looking at the map to read what we should be reaching in the next mile or two. On we went, trying to make sense of it. Maybe we were sort of seeing those things, and maybe we weren't. Finally, we gave up and decided we were on the wrong path. It was a painful conclusion because it meant we would have to push our loaded bikes back up a long, steep hill. But we did.

Once back on top, an hour later, we immediately saw the right (now left) turn toward the vestige of a fence post; we had been so busy dodging rocks and roots the first time that we had missed it. Finally back on course, we angled down a hill so steep that Mel immediately dismounted and started walking. I, however, accepted the challenge of riding it. Within thirty seconds my rear tire, carrying 25 pounds of gear, flew over my head as I executed a forward somersault. Stunned but not injured, I got up and walked down the hill with Mel. *Maybe on the next trip I'll wear a bicycle helmet. Or maybe not.*

We rode through creeks, across cattle guards, out of Beaverhead-Deerlodge National Forest, and finally into Wise River. Barney, who had arrived four hours earlier, showed us our campsite for the night: a grassy area behind a café/bar/motel complete with a dog that followed us everywhere.

We awakened to our last full day of riding, and an easy one. I got off to a bumpy start, waking up at 6:15, packing all the gear inside my tent, and then stepping outside. It was very dark, and Mel and Barney were still asleep. *What's wrong with this picture?*

With reading glasses and a flashlight, I looked again at my watch and discovered it was something past 3:15. I sighed, unpacked and crawled back into my sleeping bag.

Once on the road we climbed 29 gentle miles on a paved National Scenic Byway, drinking in the beautiful valley below. A dusty road bumped us several miles down to Elkhorn Hot Springs, where we grabbed a cabin and called it an early day. On the front porch, we aired out our camping gear, which we wouldn't need again, and took a long, languid dip in the hot springs. There we met a biker from Indiana who had just quit his job as city planner and was going to ride the entire distance to Mexico by himself while he figured out what to do with the rest of his life.

He was one of several people we met during the trip. Of the dozen or so bikers, he was the only one who approached being even half our average age of 58. Most were students who had the summer off. One was a hiker—his trail name was Incense—who was very bent over while carrying a 50-pound pack and leaning on a surprisingly short walking stick

Under threatening skies, we sprang out of the hot springs and hustled back to our cabin to move all our gear inside just before the skies opened in earnest. In the restaurant that evening we smugly watched the rain pour down as we topped off a fine meal with peach pie ala mode.

In the morning, we mounted up and rode south on a gravel

road. Reaching the tiny town of Polaris marked the end of Map 1 (of 6) of the Great Divide Ride. We cycled a few more miles (starting Map 2) to reach a convenient junction about 60 miles west of Dillon, Montana. There Barney's daughter picked us up and drove us back to Eureka, where Barney had parked his pickup truck at the start of our trip. Then he drove us home to Ellensburg.

A touch over 500 miles down, and a touch under 2000 to go. We've learned a lot and will do better next time. I can hardly wait.

9 GREAT DIVIDE RIDE II

My first taste of the Great Divide Ride made me hungry for more. And it started me thinking about how I wanted to have fun during summers. Summer was prime time for races and adventure runs on mountain trails because that was the only reliable time those trails were open. Yet the same reason—summer heat—that opened those trails also made many summer runs difficult. Most everyone—certainly including me—suffered running in the heat.

An extreme example is the Badwater 135-mile race in Death Valley, in July, going from the lowest point in the Western Hemisphere (282 feet *below* sea level at Badwater Basin) to the portal (at 8360 feet) of the trail leading to the summit of Mt. Whitney, at 14,505 feet, the highest point in the lower 48 states. Even worse, the course is entirely on pavement, where ground temperatures reach as high as 135 degrees. It is so hot that runners take care to run on the white line on the edge of the road, where it is noticeably cooler, so that glue and other parts of their running shoes don't melt.

People training for Badwater have to spend considerable time heat training—traveling to warm-weather places to run, wearing extra layers of clothing while training, exercising in saunas. It isn't for me; the percentage of time training and racing that is fun is just too small for my taste. Different strokes for different folks.

But biking in the summer is different. Yes, we still draw hot days, as we found out on our first Great Divide Ride. But I'd learned that things are a little easier on a bicycle: you can coast in places; you move at a faster pace and generate a cooling breeze around yourself; and when you aren't racing, you can take your own sweet time when you need to. *Maybe summer is the time for me to bike. I can still run the rest of the year, when it is cooler.*

By the summer after our first ride, I was ready to take another bite out of the Great Divide Ride. But I couldn't. Mel, tired of retirement (from the U.S. Foreign Service) joined the Peace Corps and was assigned to Ukraine.

The following summer, with Mel still overseas, Barney and I decided we needed to get on with the ride. We would resume pedaling from where we had finished two years earlier and cycle the next 500 miles southeast along the Continental Divide. (After he returned, Mel did this section by himself to get caught up.)

Barney and I drove from Ellensburg to Bannack, once the territorial capitol of Montana and now a restored ghost town with more than fifty buildings. We camped along Grasshopper Creek, where gold was discovered in 1862, and figured out how, between us, to cover the eight miles north to the junction where we had finished riding two years earlier.

We decided that one of us would drive north, leave the car, and cycle back to Bannack while the other would bike north and drive the car back. Barney said that since my bicycle was easier to remove from the rack, I should pedal north while he drove there. As Barney drove away in his car, it began to rain. I soon discovered I was also cycling into a stiff north wind. When we passed each other, pedaling in opposite directions, Barney was smiling and I wasn't. *Now I know why he's a Dean at my school and I'm not.*

We set up camp at Bannack and drove into Dillon for a restaurant meal. A local recommended steak and fries at the Longhorn Saloon. The food tasted great going down, but the grease churned in my stomach for hours as I lay in my tent.

In the morning, we left Barney's car (which his daughter would pick up later) at Bannack and bicycled south on a washboard dirt and gravel road built in 1862 to connect the gold rush town of Bannack to the Union Pacific Railroad in Corrine, Utah. We looked forward to a nice tailwind but drew a stiff headwind instead. *Go figure.*

In the wide open spaces of Big Sky Country, we passed an elk farm and watched several dozen elk, many with massive racks.

Starting at 6000 feet, we continued to climb under increasingly dark clouds. Suddenly an afternoon thunderstorm erupted and drove us under trees for cover. Barney changed into his full-body rain suit while I donned my $8 plastic jacket and stayed in shorts. After a few minutes, cooling rapidly, I dashed out of the trees and into a huge horse trailer hitched to an empty pickup truck parked nearby and was amazed at the abundant sleeping quarters and other amenities inside.

Once the rain stopped, we resumed riding and I stopped shivering. Late in the long day, we climbed Medicine Lodge-Sheep Creek Divide at 8000 feet. My adrenalin was flowing, and I needed every drop. Barney hit the wall and walked his bicycle up the final, steepest grade. He declared that he had just set a new record for being tired.

Finally descending into a remote area, we looked for a place—any place—to camp. We spotted a creek trickling by a few old, deserted ranch buildings. As I peered into the opening that once was a window in a long-ago cabin, a swallow flew out, giving me a facial, while a rat scurried under my feet. I suggested we camp outside, near the creek, just upstream from some milling cattle. After 48 miles we slumped into our tents.

What a difference a day makes. The next morning we broke camp, climbed a few small hills, and spotted pronghorn antelope, including a baby. Many of them, about 300 yards to our right, kept their distance while racing us across the sagebrush land as we cruised a gentle, downhill dirt road, enjoying a nice tailwind. We reached Big Sheep Canyon, which locals claim has the best trout fishing in the country. Fly fishermen and women dotted the sparkling creek for 25 eye-candy miles.

The weather was calm and overcast. Barney was rejuvenated and rode strongly into Lima, population 265, where we sat down to eat lasagna at the only café in town. The road out of town was mostly flat and wound through canyons and valleys with wide vistas. We met two cattle drives, headed up by traditional and four-wheel cowboys. One told us that yesterday's rainstorm turned the nearby Ruby River red from the clay soil.

We watched pelicans and ducks and heard sand hill cranes as we cycled past Lima Reservoir Dam. After 64 mellow miles, rain arrived, but we had already set up camp and just crawled into our tents. Raindrops and Wolverine Creek sang us to sleep.

Another overcast morning and a roller-coaster road brought us into Lakeview, population 8, where we gladly accepted a local man's offer to cook us lunch. The food was welcome, but his cooking was so bad that I could think of only three Ellensburg restaurants that would readily hire him.

We pedaled along Red Rock Lakes National Wildlife Refuge, 40,000 acres of wetlands, coniferous forests and sage plains. The area was home to moose, sand hill cranes (which we saw), trumpeter swans, pronghorn antelope and many other critters. Next, we crossed the Continental Divide at 7100-foot Red Rock Pass, bade a fond farewell to Montana, and entered the Targhee National Forest.

Idaho welcomed us with rain, thunder and lightning. I've lived in the upper Midwest and well know what such storms are like, but I must say that this one was very impressive. Three times the intense rain drove us off the dirt road to seek shelter as we tried to ride the final eighteen miles of the day. The third time, chilled and with lightning flashing all around us, Barney and I huddled under trees and separated so that one of us might live to tell the other one's widow what happened.

I was on the verge of hypothermia when I heard human shrieks. Suddenly three groups of howling teenagers on ATVs blasted through a huge water hole nearby, sending a wet, brown wall cascading over me and my two-wheeled steed. *No point trying to stay dry now.*

The storm raged, dumping a full inch of rain, as we pedaled the final, muddy miles into Island Park. After 58 miles of riding, we gratefully took a dry motel room and left a generous tip for the poor person who would have to clean it the next day. *Never again do I want to hear "Raindrops Keep Falling on My Head."*

We woke up needing to take an easy day. We pedaled out of town on an old Union Pacific Rails to Trails spur line. Part of the

Yellowstone volcanic caldera, the railroad bed had sandy soil, sometimes a bit deep, and was soggy from yesterday's downpour. As we rode the 30-mile section, passing wetlands, I identified a snorting sound ahead as coming from a moose (though I had never seen nor heard one before). Barney said it was a cow. A minute later we passed an upset cow.

We bicycled through a timber-supported tunnel and made a stunning descent for several miles along the Warm River, one of the prettiest canyons we've seen, featuring a variety of conifers and fly fisherfolks trying their luck. At the bottom we crossed the river and rode onto the Mesa Falls National Scenic Byway for a few paved miles.

Evening brought us to Squirrel Creek Ranch, population single digits. We spent the evening strolling through the elk ranch and gabbing with locals. The owner explained that velvet from the elk antlers used to bring high prices as an aphrodisiac. "But that market," he said sadly, "has been decimated by Viagra."

In response to his concerns about the local drought, Barney announced that he and I were Rain Men. On cue, the rains came, a million-dollar blessing to the area. As we crawled into our tents, the skies opened further, with a sound and light show that increased the value of our services to three million dollars.

I awakened in the morning to discover that the real function of my ground cloth was to collect a small lake under my tent. As we waited for breakfast at Squirrel Creek Ranch, the cook told us she'd arrived there from Las Vegas five days ago and was just learning to cook. Her biggest challenge, she said, was timing. She explained that a couple days earlier, when seven customers ordered eggs, she cooked and served the meals one at a time. We waited an hour for our omelets and were grateful we were the only two eating.

Our legs worked hard pedaling the water-soaked, muddy road. We celebrated each mile, whistling along at 4.5 celebrations per hour. A flattened Coors can nailed to a post welcomed us into Wyoming.

We crossed the northern flank of the Teton Mountains at 7500-foot Calf Creek and skirted the southern boundary of Yellowstone Park. All around were the charred remains of the massive 1988 fire that, according to the boys at the Squirrel Creek Ranch last night, could have been put out by "three men and three shovels" if the National Park Service had allowed them into the Park. Farther ahead was Flagg Ranch, now a large guest lodge.

Dirt suddenly morphed into pavement, changing solitude into chaos as motor homes and other vehicles shot past. The John D. Rockefeller, Jr. Parkway linked Yellowstone Park with the Grand Teton National Park, which owed much of its land to the sneaky tactics used by John D., mostly in the 1930s, to buy up land and then give it to the government.

Late afternoon brought thunder, lightning and rain. *This is a recording.* The skies emptied and then cleared as we pedaled to Colter Bay on Jackson Lake. Our site at a large campground gave us a picture-postcard view of the Tetons, so named by a lonely group of French-Iriquois trappers, who called them "les Trois Tetons," meaning "the Three Breasts."

A dry night and clear morning. *Maybe our weather luck is turning.* A smooth road took us out of the Grand Teton National Park and east onto the paved TransAmerica Bicycle Trail (here Highway 287). There we met a couple in their 60s from Illinois who put our trip in perspective. They were over halfway on their 11,000-mile, seven-month bicycle tour around the country. He grumbled that he was having trouble keeping up with his wife.

RV and SUV traffic on the paved road was jarring at first, but in ten minutes I went from nervous to blasé. By 9:30 a.m., we were eating pie ala mode and drinking ten-cent coffee at the Buffalo Valley Café, served by a waiter in desperate need of math skills. Barney, the mathematician, kindly helped her figure out our tab.

A few miles later I blundered, riding ahead of Barney and waiting for him in a shady spot just off the road. After twenty minutes or so, when I didn't see him, I rode back toward him. I continued for four miles, and then stopped a motorist coming from behind who told me she had seen someone dressed like him riding the other way. *I must have missed seeing him pass me, and he didn't see me in the shade.*

I turned around and gave chase, finally catching Barney just before he reached the Cowboy Village Resort. There we enjoyed a room and took long, languid soaks in the tub to pacify nether regions sorely taxed from the day's net climb of nearly 3000 feet.

We began riding the next morning under a crystal clear sky carrying the sun on our left and a half moon high on our right. We gulped thin mountain air and climbed nine miles to cross the Continental Divide at 9660-foot Togwotee Pass, named for a Shoshone Indian guide. On top, the highest point of our trip that year, we met a couple from New Zealand pedaling the Great Divide Ride from south to north—except instead of starting at the Mexican border, they had started in Argentina. They had no residence and had been touring on their bicycles for five years.

We began a 21-mile descent. I appreciated Barney's eye for wildlife, honed by many years of hunting, as he pointed out two moose ambling in a nearby meadow. We stopped at the Tie Hack Memorial, which honored men who had made railroad ties and floated them down the Big Wind River to help build the first transcontinental railroad. We continued to scream downhill, leaving Shoshone National Forest and coasting much of the way. I experienced the joy of cruising at 38 miles per hour wearing nothing above my waist but sunglasses and a smile.

My smile vanished when we reached the bottom and turned onto a dusty road for a long uphill grunt. Storm clouds and thunder prowled the sky but moved on, seeking other victims. The climb steepened. My lungs burned, my back ached, and my butt was numb. I swore softly as each curve revealed a new section to climb. A final pound of flesh brought us to a lovely alpine meadow.

On spent legs, we biked through those meadows *down* to 9210-foot Union Pass, crossing the Continental Divide at the junction of three mountain ranges—Wind River, Absaroka and Gros Ventre. The road continued past Lake of the Woods and flattened out.

After 52 miles, too many in granny (lowest) gear, we camped by Strawberry Creek. Up went a bear bag since we were in grizzly country. Two years earlier, Barney had donated $100 to support the Great Divide Ride project and in return had gotten a mile designated with his name. Tonight we camped alone on the mile he chose, near where he had worked with the Forest Service decades ago. Over supper, he told me stories of this land.

We awakened, as usual, a bit before 6 a.m. We ate and loaded our bikes in virtual silence, savoring the 9000-foot solitude. The cool morning floated along for a few miles.

Then reality bit. Even small hills brought protests from

overworked muscles, as the bill for yesterday's hard work came due. I hadn't been eating enough, and for a couple of hours I mentally checked out. I was a zombie on wheels as we mechanically rode the Green River drainage and left Bridger National Forest.

Finally we reached the only café of the day and discovered it was closed, permanently. Some nutritious trail food (Okay, Cheetos) revived me for a couple hours until we reached Cora, which had a historic post office but no other services. It was only 4 p.m., and only eleven miles into Pinedale, which had full services, but we just didn't have enough energy to ride there.

The postmistress in Cora let us camp in the weeds nearby. For the day we somehow covered 47 miles and the weather was nice. *Sorry. I'm just too tired to remember anything else.*

Thank God (literally) for new days to give us fresh starts. Barney pedaled the pavement into Pinedale (population 1180) while I churned the alternate route featuring four miles of soft gravel. *Why do things the easy way when you can do them the hard way?*

On a Saturday morning, we arrived just in time to watch Pinedale celebrate its annual Rendezvous Days. First we found a pancake breakfast, hosted by the good folks at the Community United Church of Christ, where I forked mounds of food through sun-blistered lips into an empty body. Next, since no one sat within two tables of us, Barney and I retired to a local Laundromat for aqueous fumigation of our clothes and bodies.

As our clothes dried, we stepped outside and watched a parade go by, 35 minutes celebrating the Mountain Man and Indian heritage of the area. When that show ended, a fair broke out. Tables sprang up along Main Street offering everything from cotton candy to cowboy hats. The parade Mountain Men sat at tables, sipping their lattes.

At a grocery store, we visited with a philosophy professor who had led a group up Mt. Rainier and in 1976-77 had backpacked the entire Continental Divide Trail, some of it (in Colorado) on cross-country skis. He was working summers here as a ranger, bringing his pair of llamas from California to carry his load on long hikes.

Barney exited town on the paved, flat 13-mile road to Boulder, our destination for the night. I stayed to watch the 65th annual Green River Rendezvous Pageant on the rodeo grounds at the edge of town. The 75-minute program depicted the history of the area and featured fur traders, Indians and missionaries. Music came from a group known informally as "The Young and the Rest of Us," the "Young" being a local 14-year-old who was the junior national fiddler champion.

After the show, I cycled the same route as Barney to Boulder, population 75. The paved cruise on a wide shoulder with a strong tailwind on a lightly clouded afternoon was fifty minutes of sheer pleasure. Along the way, an osprey circled high above its massive nest atop a telephone pole.

Boulder's motel—all seven rooms—was full, mostly rented to drillers enjoying the boom in oil and gas exploration. I found Barney down by a tributary of the Green River at a pretty campsite where we plunked down for the night.

We awakened to the pitter-patter of raindrops on our tents. From a van that had arrived during the night, a man emerged with a fishing rod, looking for breakfast. He talked about a natural gas rig nearby that had recently blown up, killing two drillers. "But we'll be alright," he said, "as long as Bush is President."

Raindrops chased us as we rode. Soon gray clouds surrounded us and we surrendered, ducking into a cattle shed whose tin roof rang from the downpour. I wore every piece of clothing I had as we waited out the storm.

Back on the road, we watched swallows swoop and loop through their aerial acrobatics in the freshly scrubbed air whose ground-level ozone gave off a scent of newly washed bed sheets. The washboard road led us up through a rocky, treeless area, and into a fierce afternoon thunderstorm. Ahead of Barney, I dismounted and pressed against a huge rock, curling under my meager rain jacket and taking a pounding. When rain gave way to hail, I became a child, counting to 100 over and over again to make it all go away.

It worked. After thirty minutes the storm passed. Now feeling vulnerable, I waited for Barney. When he finally rode around a curve and came into view, he told me his story. During the storm he had crammed his body into a large crack in a large rock, and took his beating. Afterwards he discovered, and then had to repair, a flat back tire.

We cycled south toward increasingly dark skies. Mud flew off our front wheels and onto our faces and bodies. Vehicles rushed toward us, fleeing the area we were approaching. At Little Sandy Creek, we scouted for a protected place to camp as the storm struck. The sky unleashed driving rain and a furious display of thunder and lightning, sometimes only two seconds apart.

We did the best we could. Barney found a small space under a tree while I crammed my tent into a narrow, cow-pie-covered space between two trees. We tried to sleep, surrounded by frequent piercings of light and the loudest thunder I've ever heard. *This was supposed to be an easy day—38 miles—but it wasn't.*

The wind howled most of the night, making me grateful my tent was so low to the ground. Eventually the wind chased away the clouds and we woke up to a clear, sun-kissed morning. Despite the beautiful start to the day, I wrapped everything on my bicycle in plastic. *I've learned this lesson the hard way.*

We broke camp for the last time and cycled an undulating road across the 8000-foot desert of southeastern Wyoming. Barney rode strongly, smelling the barn. As he powered up hills I could hear the crowd roar: "You Da Man." But no one else was there—just the two of us—as for two miles we cruised along the crest of the Continental Divide, enjoying splendid views into the huge basins on each side. *Life is good.*

The ride was easy. When we reached a short section of pavement and, thus, civilization, my eyes scanned the horizon, spotting bottles and cans instead of antelope. A strong tailwind propelled us to the end of our adventure at South Pass, our third crossing of the Continental Divide for the day. Because this pass is the easiest gap through the Rocky Mountains, it was the main passage in the 1800s for wagon trains going west. After 33 miles for the day, and 500 for our entire trip, we stopped at South Pass City, population 8, a historic remnant of a gold mining town dating from 1865.

In front of a tiny store, we waited for Barney's daughter to pick us up. A 10th grade boy, the only resident who wasn't an adult, told us about his daily, forty-mile bus commute (each way) to school at Lander, and how the snow was twenty-one feet deep here two winters ago. He loved the place.

A BLM official stopped by and took pictures of Barney and me to present at a regional meeting. When he asked why I wasn't wearing a helmet, I just couldn't think of anything to say except: "Mamas, don't let your babies grow up to be cowboys." *Pretty lame, I know.*

Barney's daughter arrived and drove us to Salt Lake City. She and Barney were going to a family reunion nearby, so they kindly kept my bicycle and gear and dropped me off at the Greyhound station to catch a midnight bus headed to Ellensburg. Memories of the last twelve days were flooding across my mind when a passenger asked how my summer was going. As my children used to answer, when I asked them how their day had gone, I simply replied: "Fine."

10 GREAT DIVIDE RIDE III

While Barney and I were cycling in Montana, Idaho and Wyoming, taking our daily poundings from thunderstorms, Mel was in Ukraine, awash in vodka and working with locals engaged in shady business dealings. Mel was good with vodka, but not with corruption. So by the next summer he had resigned from the Peace Corps and returned to Ellensburg, ready to join Barney and me to take our third bite out of the Great Divide Ride.

Barney and I had learned a few things when we rode without Mel, so we made some changes. My mechanical skills, lower even than Mel's and Barney's, rivaled those of a rabbit (no offense to rabbits intended), so I made a deal with Fred at our local bicycle shop: he'd give me my bike in excellent working condition in return for my money and my promise that I wouldn't try to "fix" anything.

Barney, newly retired, abandoned the trailer he'd been pulling. All three of us now carried our gear in panniers (saddle bags) on "hard tail" mountain bikes that had front, but not rear, suspension forks. Barney's and mine also sported suspension seat posts to pamper our posteriors, and both front and rear racks (and panniers) to balance the load and give us more room to carry water across the desert section this year. And after getting bombed with rain last year, I carried a serious new rain suit that Laurae had bought for me. Mel, nonchalant as always, made few changes and headed out with pretty much the same gear he had three years earlier.

Mel picked me up to drive 1000 miles to meet Barney at 3 p.m. the next day in South Pass City, Wyoming, where our ride had ended last year. Getting ready to leave a gas station near Lewiston, Idaho, we observed Mel's keys dangling inside his locked car. Two policewomen, one cowboy, one casino worker, two coat hangers, no dollars and 45 minutes later (don't ask), we were on our way.

Seeking lodging that night in Dillon, Montana, we inquired at an old hotel. The grizzled clerk looked at us and said they had no rooms. We moved on to a semi-seedy motel whose proprietor told us we were lucky we didn't stay at that hotel. When we pressed him for details, his eyes rolled but his lips didn't move.

The next morning, rolling down the road by 7 a.m., we drove to South Pass City, arriving there just before 3 p.m., ten minutes after Barney had arrived.

The area has a rich history. When gold was discovered along

Willow Creek in 1865, this second oldest city in Wyoming briefly boomed. The Oregon, Mormon and Pony Express Trails, which provided passage for 350,000 people heading west in the mid-1800s, converge here. A few miles away stands a memorial to the Willie Handcart Company disaster, where 67 Mormons died in a severe October snowstorm. Indeed, the Oregon-Mormon Trail has been called, according to Barney, "the longest graveyard in America."

Barney, Mel and I saddled up and started pedaling southeast. Behind us, white smoke billowed from fresh fires in Utah, while ahead of us lay a haze created by Colorado fires. After four miles, when Mel stopped to deal with his flat tire, he discovered that he had brought spare inner tubes with the wrong type of valve that wouldn't fit into his wheel. While we patched his flat, we discovered we had already missed a turn. As we rode back to get on course, I bet Mel $5 I wouldn't get a flat tire the entire trip. Barney declined to get in on the action.

As we pumped up short, sharp hills, I felt a light burning in my lungs, a reminder we were at 7000 feet. We kissed our last tree for 140 miles good-bye and camped at a pretty spot along the Clearwater River, our only certain water source for the next two days. There Mel discovered his water filter didn't work well and his ancient, one-gallon water container was leaking.

We scratched our heads since we each needed to carry two

to three gallons (16-24 pounds) of water to get across the desert. Soon we were scratching elsewhere as mosquitoes drove us into our tents for the night.

At dawn, we resumed riding, starting the two days I feared the most of the entire 2500-mile ride. Here the Continental Divide splits into two ridges surrounding the Great Divide Basin, a high desert (100 miles east to west by 50 miles north to south) where water travels neither to the Atlantic nor Pacific Ocean, but drains straight into the thirsty ground.

We knew of three possible water sources for the day. After twelve miles, we found the first, an artesian well, and topped off our supplies. There we met an older man and woman, their grandchild and another child. For years they had been camping here for the summer, living in a trailer and supervising 1800-2000 cattle grazing by permit on public and private lands. They told us about intense lightning strikes nearby. They'd never seen a rattlesnake here; the most dangerous animals were badgers. As we left, they wished us luck with temperatures that would soar into the high 90s.

Blessed with a tailwind, we made good time on the flat road, dirt with gravel except for sudden sandy spots that made us fishtail. After more than forty miles, we spotted Crooks Mountain and Green Mountain in the distance, but barely noticed crossing the Continental Divide. As the miles passed through flat, desolate desert and the temperature soared, Mel, normally our strongest rider, was struggling. We stopped, gave him sugar, water and electrolytes, and got him to lie down in a dry creek bed (the only kind we'd seen) while we rigged a canopy to shade him.

After thirty minutes, he said he was ready to try riding again. Two miles down the road, his tire went flat. New patches went on. We struggled in the heat, taking frequent rest breaks. Finally, we reached the second water source, a ranch. The buildings were locked, no one was home, and we found no water. We rode on, depleting our water but trying to make it last until we reached the third source, a reservoir where we would camp.

After seventy miles, and twelve hours in the blazing sun, we reached A & M Reservoir. It was bone dry. Barney and Mel, declaring they were too tired to do anything else, dismounted and lay inert in the dirt. After a few minutes, they got up and did what they must to set up their tents. With no water to cook supper, we just crumpled off to sleep, hungry, thirsty and worried about what we would do the next day.

As I lay in my tent, surrounded by sagebrush in the hot, dry middle of nowhere, I kept thinking about a guy in a pickup truck, the only person we'd seen the entire day after the first twelve miles. His words when we briefly met, many hours ago, haunted me: "I wouldn't be caught dead out here today."

We rose, well before dawn, ate nothing, and started riding in silence as soon as we could sort of see our way using flashlights. We needed cool miles because we were long out of water. The irony struck me: *Last year, Barney and I were deluged by thundershowers day after day; now, every drop is precious.*

We studied the map and changed our route, giving ourselves three new, possible places to find water. Three miles down a terrible, rocky, sandy road we reached the first one. Wild mustangs and antelope watched as we discovered that Lost Soldier Creek, unlike all the "creeks" we had passed yesterday, was flowing. We grinned like kids at Christmas as we opened our gift. *We are saved.*

With bulging bottles, we continued pedaling that same, now marvelous, road. Mel rode on the left and Barney on the right as befitted their politics. I belonged in the middle, since anyone whose opinions differ from mine is an extremist.

A few hours later, Mel's tire lost its final puff of air as we pulled into Lamont, population three (Grandma, Grandpa and their grandchild), which consisted entirely of Grandma's Café. We were grateful for food, even Grandma's French toast. *Apparently she's English.* After breakfast we put patches (#4 and #5 if you're counting) on Mel's decrepit inner tube, which went flat half a mile down the road. Back to Grandma's for #6.

A few miles later, we rejoined the official route and crossed the Continental Divide for the 13th time since leaving the Canadian border. We rode into Rawlins, a blue-collar town of 9000 people whose vacant buildings were a legacy from their 1980s boom in uranium mining. Long ago, Rawlins (and its jail) had been home to Martha Jane Canary, better known as Calamity Jane, a Wild West Bad Girl.

We found a cheap motel and cheered as Mel threw away his pathetic, multipatched inner tube and inserted a newly purchased one coated with Slime and having the right kind of valve. As we fell asleep, I thought about lessons from the last two days: *despite all our plans and precautions, we have to accept problems as they arise, deal with them, and keep going; getting upset is a waste of energy; patience is indeed a virtue.*

After breakfast in town, we stocked up on food, our last chance for three days, ducked under Interstate 80, and climbed south out of Rawlins into an overcast morning. The land was desolate but our spirits were high. We no longer feared dehydration; in fact, we feared nothing. The Three Amigos were back in business.

Three times we met lone backpackers hiking the Continental Divide Trail south to north as we cruised along the flat terrain. Mel had regained his appetite and strength while Barney, who had shed 20 pounds and 100 points off his blood cholesterol level before the ride, had a new bike, carried less gear and continued to ride strongly. He also sported a new gps (global positioning system) unit, a retirement gift he was learning to use. Its readings, from four to ten satellites, gave us elevations and locations that fit well with our map.

The paved, roller-coaster road soon turned into a gravel washboard as the desert rose to meet the Sierra Madre Range. We climbed across the Continental Divide at 8000-foot Middlewood Hill as on the horizon appeared something we hadn't seen for days: trees.

We descended 700 feet and camped by a small creek. To tell the truth, even after studying the map and Barney's gps, we weren't sure which of two possible creeks it was. But it didn't matter. Although the temperature again rose into the 90s, a sudden afternoon breeze blew through camp, releasing heat from our baked bodies as thunder pealed nearby. We retired along our unknown creek as a few raindrops kissed us good-night.

I woke up to Papa Antelope screaming at Mel, whose tent apparently was blocking access to his favorite watering hole. Over breakfast, Mel, a veteran biker, announced that he had his first ever saddle sore. He anointed himself (neither Barney nor I would do it) with Bag Balm.

For five miles, the flat altitude profile on our map masked a succession of hills. The surface suddenly, wonderfully, morphed into a "primitive" (ungraveled, and thus smoother) dirt road. Water was abundant again as we pedaled into the Medicine Bow

National Forest. Aspen, pine and spruce trees provided shade while deer replaced antelope as our companions.

We took our sweet time, savoring the silent woods. The road meandered through beautiful "Aspen Alley," a narrow lane bordered by dense walls of aspens on each side, before topping out at 8200 feet. On the long, paved descent the breeze whistled through my thinning hair as I maxed out my cyclometer at 40 miles per hour, after which it died.

We ducked into a ranch building as an afternoon thunderstorm came calling. Afterwards, we rode the alternate route in the Little Snake River (unrelated to *the* Snake River) valley, a beautiful area zigzagging the Wyoming/Colorado border. Among the impressive dude and trophy ranches, top prize went to Three Forks Ranch, owned by the same David Porter who owned the St. Louis Cardinals baseball team.

Along the river we camped at a picture-postcard setting. While I repaired my cyclometer (people who know me would find this hard to believe), Mel read Larry McMurtry and Barney chose Tom Clancy. We slept under the stars, listening to water music.

Now in Colorado, we began the next day pedaling a 1400-foot climb up a gravel road. The morning was cool, our legs were fresh, and we were young. *Would you believe two out of three?* Despite the intense grades, Mel stubbornly refused to use his granny (lowest) gear, a gear Barney and I had come to know and love.

Tom drove by in his pickup truck and invited us to stop by the next place, a few miles down the road, and see Darlene if we wanted water or anything else. Being neighborly guys, Mel and I stopped when we reached there an hour later. Darlene sported a very short haircut as she greeted us at the door with her robe almost on. After a few minutes of chatting, Mel and I declined her kind offer of water "or anything else" and rode on to catch up with Barney.

We passed old cabins, sheep, meadows and mountains in the Routt National Forest. At Columbine, a lady pointed out two columbines (the state flower), the only ones we would see the entire trip because of the drought. There we learned that our intended camping spot for the night wasn't open, so we shortened the day's ride and camped at Steamboat Lake, part of Colorado's park system.

For the first time on our trip, we camped near other people. We drew the busiest week-end of the year, the marina teeming with boaters and swimmers. Barney and Mel left to eat at a nearby restaurant while I cooked supper in camp and then walked over to the amphitheatre to catch a slide show on local wildflowers.

The speaker, 85-year-old Rilla Wiggens, soon made it clear that she had no use for Texans or hippies. A nearby couple directed their three young children to sit next to me on a long log. During the program the kids kicked dust, each other, and me while occasionally tripping over and disconnecting the slide projector cord. Their parents hissed at them from behind, but they were hard to hear because the man next to them was trying to calm three large, whining dogs parked at his feet while we all swatted mosquitoes.

The slides were good, too.

We awakened to the idyllic sound of an SUV alarm detonating nearby, perhaps to ward off an invading chipmunk. We cycled a few miles and finally found good French toast at the Dutch Creek Guest Ranch, though Barney claimed his recipe was better.

We crashed down a winding, oiled, gravel road. Without a shirt, cap or helmet (but with paid-up life insurance), I beat the posted speed limit (25 mph) by double digits as we shot into Clark, which consisted of a store. There Barney guzzled Gatorade, I swigged Diet Coke, and Mel downed a caramel roll with something he'd been missing for days—espresso. Mel's fuel proved superior as he dropped Barney and me when we resumed riding along the Elk River.

A swarm of grasshoppers welcomed us as we rolled into Steamboat Springs and found a motel room. Although the town is famous for world class skiing and ski jumping combined with Stetson hats, tourists also flock here in the summer for hiking, fly fishing, mountain biking and other outdoor activities. After a relaxing afternoon just being tourists, we called it a day. I won the rock-paper-scissors game and got a bed to myself.

Two easy days had refreshed us. Now we faced a forty-mile day with a net gain of 2200 feet. At our motel's continental breakfast we met Paul, a genial gentleman from Peoria, who said he had "never had a bad day in my life." He showed us the small crescent wrench he always carried and said he's "70," then (a little later) "69," then (a little later yet) "69 in a few months." I wondered at what age we return to the tendency we had as children to exaggerate our age, reversing the tendency, in our middle years, to minimize our age.

As we rode south out of town, the angle of the rising sun gave my shadow long legs astride a tall bicycle. *I like it.* We soon left pavement, whose miles flowed by so easily it almost felt like cheating to count them. A one-lane dirt road wound through a lovely valley following the Yampa River upstream. We crossed a dam that had created Stagecoach Reservoir from the river, and then rode the single-track Elk Run Trail along the water before heading steadily upward for eighteen miles.

We passed beautiful, solitary homes deep in the woods and wondered why we spend so many tax dollars saving them from the inevitable forest fires. After lunch in a shady spot, Mel napped while Barney and I resumed the climb, finally reaching our campground at 8900-foot Lynx Pass. Mel eventually found us there.

Our final climb proved surprisingly easy as the usual afternoon thunder bumped through, bringing cloud cover and cooling, but no significant rain. During the night, though, a storm caught us by surprise. We jumped out of our warm, dry sleeping bags and scrambled out in the dark to secure rain flies onto our tents amid rain, thunder and lightning. *The joys of camping.*

After a nippy night, we rose early, packed our slightly soggy gear, and rode. Soon we parted company for the day. Barney chose the paved TransAmerican Bicycle Route (Highway 40 here) to Kremmling while Mel and I traveled there by dirt.

We left Barney, forded a creek that was lower than usual, and then began, according to our map commentary, "one of the most dramatic dives on the entire Great Divide Ride." The views were spectacular as we plunged 1700 feet in three miles through a state wildlife area featuring pinon pines and junipers. We arrived in Radium with wrists sore from squeezing our smoking brakes.

Radium, a railroad outpost devoid of public services, is a BLM recreation area. Here the Colorado River carried people starting and finishing their catered raft tours. Mel and I found a little shade and reloaded our water bottles for the long, hot climb out of the valley. Near a telephone, I noticed an abandoned can of Coke three-quarters full and took a drink. I tasted warm Coke and a mouthful of cigarette ashes.

The climb out took its toll, but finally we reached Inspiration Point on top, which rewarded us with fine views of the Gore Canyon below. We coasted down into Kremmling to meet Barney, who had beaten us there by three hours. I felt a little guilty taking a motel room, but enjoyed cleaning up and eating someone else's cooking.

After supper, strolling through the small downtown and back to our motel, we spotted four guys drinking beer by a pickup truck. One of them teed up a golf ball and drove it straight down Main Street. I heard no sound of impact as the ball apparently threaded its way between vehicles parked on both sides of the street. *Yes, Colorado has good ol' boys.*

In the morning, we faced another uphill day, but short, one of two easy days to our finish line. Before ordering breakfast, we asked for separate checks. Our sleepy waitress looked at the three of us and asked, "How many?" I served coffee to the customers, but forgot to serve our waitress, who desperately needed it.

Mel hugged the edge of a narrow, shoulderless road out of town when a man in a black Jeep passed within inches of him and yelled at him to get off the road. Mel replied in sign language. After we crossed a serene section of the Colorado River, Barney became the biker version of Kojak, sucking on a Lollipop as he cruised up the smooth, gentle grade. The high country in Meadow Park was pretty, but paled in comparison to yesterday's spectacular gorge.

We camped along the Williams Fork River, a popular place for pike fishing, but saw no one else. We lazed away the afternoon reading, dozing, doing crossword puzzles, and sticking our pinkies and other body parts in the river. Time passed agreeably.

Clouds and a little thunder cooled the evening as we cooked our final camp supper. My meal was a Pasta Roni concoction with Parmesan and Romano sauce followed by a Little Debbie oatmeal cookie accompanied by a fine selection of iodine-treated waters. Barney had similar fare, but selected filtered water. Mel, the gourmand, had a touch of whiskey with his meal.

A mild headache and fatigue struck me, but I thought nothing of it. Nearby signs warned of bear and moose, so we packed our food remnants away from the tents. A brief thundershower chased us into our tents for the night.

Another cold morning at altitude welcomed us to our final riding day. We had hoped to go farther on the trip this year, but wildfires south of here had forced all organized Great Divide Ride tours in Colorado and New Mexico to be canceled. Fortunately, we weren't organized (as you can probably tell), so we managed to squeeze in about 400 miles, reaching the northern edge of the Colorado fires and bumping our total distance on the Great Divide

Ride up to 1400 miles.

We grunted and gasped up to 9500-foot Ute Pass, where the view was magnificent—a vast army of rugged peaks guarding its valley. We entered Summit County, a historic gold-mining region, and slammed 1000 feet down to the valley floor. I didn't pedal a stroke for five miles as the thin mountain air iced my bare skin.

Once down, we dodged through rugged road construction areas leading into Silverthorne, a tourist town on Interstate 70. I suddenly experienced a power outage, moving in slow motion, aching all over. I thought it was altitude sickness but later learned it was a Giardia infection, probably from drinking water too soon after treating it with iodine.

Sickness nailed me, but its timing was perfect. Our trip was finished a few minutes before I was. At Silverthorne, I crawled into a motel bed and stayed there for eighteen hours.

The next day, Mel paid off his $5 bet since I hadn't had a flat tire the entire trip (nor had Barney). Barney and Mel climbed into separate cars with relatives to continue their summer fun. I hitched a ride in Mel's car to Rock Springs, Wyoming to board a bus bound for Ellensburg. I was still wobbly, but there's nothing like a 24-hour bus ride to wring out what ails you.

At Ogden, Utah, around midnight, an older man boarded the bus and sat next to me. We talked briefly, and I learned he was a veteran of the Korean War. I told him, "Thank you."

He replied, "Thank you."

Neither of us said another word as we rode into the night. It was a strangely moving moment.

11 GREAT DIVIDE RIDE IV

The next summer Barney, Mel and I had two decisions to make.
First, would we cycle the remaining 1033 miles of the Great Divide
Ride—the section between Silverton, Colorado and the Mexican
border—in one year or two? Since the starting and ending points
were a long way from home, and the logistics of getting to the
start and then home afterwards were getting more complicated,
we gulped and decided to ride it all in one summer.

The second question was: which direction should we ride?
The advantages of pedaling south were: the map's mileage and
commentary were laid out in that direction; we'd be more likely
to have tailwinds; and we had ridden the other sections in that
direction. Riding north had advantages, too: we could adapt to
lower altitudes in New Mexico before riding the high country of
Colorado; it would give more time for the Colorado snow to melt
before we arrived there; and we might scoot across New Mexico
before their monsoon season hit.

In the end, none of it mattered. We left that decision to

serendipity and Barney, our Minister of Transportation. When he found us a ride to the Mexican border, we would ride north.

The time arrived. After 24 hours and 850 miles of Greyhound hospitality, Mel and I reached central Utah, got off the bus, yawned, stretched, and piled into the back seat of Barney's waiting pickup truck loaded with all our bicycles and gear plus Barney and his relatives, Phil and Suzanne, our drivers. Another 12 hours and 650 miles brought us, at midnight, to Tucson, Arizona, where we grabbed motel rooms. The next morning, we drove another 300 miles to Antelope Wells, New Mexico, a lonely border crossing into Mexico. We unpacked the truck and thanked Phil and Suzanne as they drove away.

U.S. Customs officials—unlike those we had met at the Montana/Canadian border several years earlier—were relaxed and friendly. They warned us about rattlesnakes, wished us luck and pointed out the paved, flat road at 5700 feet heading north across the same Chihuahuan Desert that extends south almost to Mexico City. This remote, barren area, the second largest desert in North America, is notorious for drug smuggling and illegal entry into the U.S.

We mounted our bicycles and pedaled north past an old Phelps-Dodge copper mine whose company town had been purchased by Homeland Security to use for training. Dirt devils swirled around the mesquite, sage, creosote bush, Russian thistles

and wide variety of cacti. Barney, back to towing a trailer, spotted
a roadrunner that looked remarkably like its cartoon character.
Temperatures climbed into the upper 80s.

We passed animal-crossing signs with a silhouette that didn't
quite look like a cow. Mel later learned the signs were to protect
a wild herd of about 125 bison. That herd was slowly
disappearing, because when the animals wandered onto private
land, ranchers allowed hunters to shoot them for about $2500
apiece.

Late afternoon, after four hours and 46 miles, we reached
Hachita ("little hatchet"), population 40, and were welcomed at
the café by Elma, who had come here from the Philippines with
her husband more than a decade earlier. After a fine meal, we
shuffled into our tents behind the café to sleep with a few dogs
and raindrops.

Hard ground, barking dogs and strong winds made for poor
sleep. Over generous breakfast burritos the next morning, Elma
told of the old woman in town who had been bitten by a
rattlesnake; by the time an ambulance had arrived from the
nearest medical facility, fifty miles away, she had died. Elma also
told us about "illegals" heading north who subsisted on
rattlesnakes, which, they said, taste like fish.

We resumed riding. The paved road north carried many signs
that said "Dip." I tried not to take it personally. Another sign,

bullet-riddled in the ditch, said "Courtesy Pays." *Not enough, apparently.*

Two miles after the surface turned to gravel, one of Mel's tires went flat. It was a Vietnamese tire he had bought a few months earlier when he and his wife, Keiko, had bicycled 1000 miles across Vietnam and part of Cambodia. A few miles later, Mel had another flat. We changed it faster than before, proving that even at our age we were trainable.

After 37 remote miles and one gentle crossing of the Continental Divide, we passed an old ranch that real estate agents would describe as a "fixer-upper with great potential at an affordable price." Two miles later, we reached the Thorn Ranch, now the Escondida Land and Cattle Company. Mel used Spanish, one of his many languages, and sweet talk to get us permission to camp there.

We talked with Oscar and his wife, who had moved from Chihuahua, Mexico in 1987 to manage the place. Oscar told of a couple of bikers who had recently camped at the old ranch we'd passed two miles back; one had been bitten by a rattlesnake there, and his leg ballooned while Oscar had driven him an hour down the road to get medical help.

At camp, a dog escaped with Mel's Cheetos while a cat stole my Little Debbie honey bun, proving that they, too, have good taste. I retired to bed and went through my usual preventive maintenance—putting Bag Balm on my lips and butt, though not always in the correct sequence. Mel and Barney tinkered with their bicycles, which is almost always a bad idea.

Ranch dogs crooned all night. We began riding at 7 a.m., as usual, heading north on dirt. Under cloudless skies, wild horses thundered across our path. Our next road companions were cattle, including Brahman bulls, which we declined to ride.

Jackrabbit carcasses, picked clean, littered the road. Mel pointed out a female jackalope (a "jillalope?"). Later, in a museum, I saw another jackalope—a stuffed jackrabbit with antelope horns—but still didn't get it. (I finally learned that "jackalope" is an urban legend created from the appearance of jackrabbits infected with the Shope papilloma virus.)

Riding dusty roads for two days, we'd seen a total of one car while being pushed by winds coming in various flavors of south, especially southwest. We soon discovered that, unlike what we had expected, riding north here gave us mostly tailwinds. *Dumb luck on our part.* But the hills, altitude, distance and dry, desert heat were taking a toll—a little headache, sore and dry throat, burning lungs and sore muscles. *This trip will be tough.*

After 39 miles we entered Silver City, where Mel bought a tire at the only bike shop on our route for the next 800 miles. This city of 11,000 people exploded into existence in 1870 following a silver strike. Gold mining followed, and turquoise was mined nearby. But the most important metal here turned out to be copper, which originally was mined by Native Americans and used by the Mexican mint until 1845. Silver City also was home to Billy the Kid, legendary Wild West outlaw of the late 1800s.

A century ago people came to Silver City to sleep in the open air to recover from tuberculosis, but we spent the night inside a motel.

North of Silver City the terrain changed from desert into forest. A woman in town said we might not be able to continue biking because of nearby wildfires; she suggested we check with the Forest Service. Mel and I were disinclined to ask since they might say "No," but straight-arrow Barney went by the book. When he asked, he learned the fires were east of our route, so we could proceed.

We climbed out of town and passed the Chino Santa Rita Copper Mine, a vast open pit. Nearby, we dismounted and walked through an old cemetery containing graves of European immigrant miners, Hispanic miners, and their wives and children who had died here more than a century ago.

Smoke ahead came from a new forest fire that had started last night. We stopped at a Ranger Station to see if we were in danger as we headed into the Gila National Forest. It was Saturday, so the station was closed. *I guess it makes sense to keep the station closed on week-ends, when the most people are in the forest.* We rode on, secure in our ignorance.

Smoke billowed to the east and west, but our road north cut neatly between the fires. We cycled the Geronimo Trail Scenic Byway, a narrow corridor of national forest land between the Gila Wilderness of the Mogollon Mountains and the Aldo Leopold Wilderness in the Black Range. Bear, mountain lion, antelope and elk called the area home. We camped alone at Rocky Canyon Campground and its nonexistent stream. Water lay nine miles ahead, after a steep climb, but we were spent.

Sleeping at 7500 feet was cool, literally. The next morning, under another cloudless sky and in complete solitude, we tackled the climb we couldn't do last night. *You know you're going slowly when each ridge on the washboard road feels like an uphill followed by a downhill.*

For forty minutes, our bicycles operated in granny (lowest) gear until we reached the summit. We shot down to Black Canyon Campground and the first creek with water we'd seen in 180 miles. We filtered water and then pedaled up to a view described on our map as "awesome," but on top all I could see was Barney and Mel. *Close enough.*

Mel, with his long legs, was our strongest biker, but Barney was riding very well, too. He suffered slightly less than Mel and me as we rode 36 tough miles in ten hours to reach Beaverhead Work Center, where people were busy shuttling supplies and personnel to fight nearby forest fires but let us pitch our tents, right next to the helipad.

After our second climb today I had said to myself, *If there are many more of these, we'll be cooked.* There were, and we were.

With a helicopter scheduled to land next to our tents at eight the next morning, we left at seven. But not before a couple of fire fighters kindly gave us warm breakfast burritos and coffee and told us water was scarce for the next 100 miles. We rode away, accompanied by an animal sound that we in unison identified as a coyote, a cow and a bird. *At least two of us aren't ready yet for a wilderness merit badge.*

Pedaling along a valley floor in the Gila National Forest, we watched two dozen elk prance across our path. A mile later, dozens of deer followed suit. The day brought a mellow mood; we were going to enjoy this trip and take things as they came. Yesterday Mel and I had considered each hill a challenge to our manhood. Today the hills were gentler and we had nothing to prove. I spent some of my time wondering why the other side of the washboard road was always smoother—until I got on it.

A gentle breeze nudged us north while the sun warmed our sides and backs. We reached a junction. The official route on our map made two legs of a triangle, while another road was the third leg. We took the road less traveled, and it made all the difference (well, fifteen miles difference). We appreciated another fine, dry day, knowing that when the monsoon season arrives here in a few weeks, these dirt and clay roads will become a muddy nightmare.

On one descent, I simultaneously dodged rocks and swatted flies while accelerating (since swatting requires letting go of the brakes with at least one hand). Barney, in contrast, does one thing at a time. On a short, smooth hill, halfway down, Barney screeched to a halt. When I asked him if anything was wrong, he explained: "I had to scratch my head." (Admittedly, that involved removing his helmet, a complication Mel and I didn't have.)

Sandstone rock formations and dry grasslands preceded the Plains of San Augustin, a prehistoric lake bed where large craters and meteorites had been found. After too many hours, our tanks on E, we pedaled three inches inside the Apache National Forest, threw down our tents, and watched the sun set.

Morning hors d'oeuvres were a climb to sip the cool, fresh air at 8200 feet atop the Continental Divide, one of three crossings around Allegres Mountain. The next course, which we declined, was pea soup, deepening in color and flavor in a stock tank along the road. Our fine selection of beverages consisted of Gatorade and a variety of waters: tap from Silver City; pumped and filtered from Black Canyon Creek; and a special mineral variety for those who prefer the taste of iodine.

The main course—37 miles—took us into Pie Town, where the Daily Pie Café (the Pie-O-Neer Café was closed for remodeling) provided enchiladas and burgers. For dessert, we met Nita, a resident who befriends folks pedaling the Great Divide Ride. She invited us into her house to shower (after four days), wash clothes and camp on her front deck. We gladly added our names in her guest book to those of other bikers from around the world as old rock-and-roll tunes from her massive music collection and sound system reverberated throughout her house.

Nita showed us around. She drove us a mile out of town to see one of 27 dish-shaped satellite antennas. Those dishes make a huge, Y-shaped pattern known as the Very Large Array that constitutes the largest radio telescope in the world. The system receives radio waves emitted long ago by stars, galaxies and quasars, and has been used as a backdrop for movies such as *Contact*.

Our nightcap was another trip to the Daily Pie for catfish. Since we three were splitting the bill (treating Nita), my colleagues financially forced me to follow suit when they ordered three-berry pie ala mode. We went to sleep on Nita's porch, watching the beautiful sunset, knowing its red color came from fire smoke.

Back to the Daily Pie for breakfast. I ordered Freedom Toast since "French" ain't spoken 'round here. We sat one mile from where a bicyclist had recently been killed during the Race Across America, when, sleep-deprived and deep in the night, he had crossed into the path of an oncoming truck.

Our initial impression of Pie Town, population sixty, improved as we talked with longtime and recent residents who loved the solitude, low prices and mild summers here. Joe, the cook, took pride in his work—with good reason. Suddenly two grizzled hombres straight out of the Old West walked in. One packed a huge knife in his sheath while the other packed heat, probably a .45. We readily agreed with everything they said. After we finished breakfast and left, we upgraded the town's status to that of a *friendly* dump.

Whether it was the sand or last night's catfish, we frequently fishtailed in the dirt as we pedaled north. Barney took many short breaks and in effect set the pace. Mel took longer, less frequent breaks. We rode our separate patterns, playing leap-frog but staying within a few miles of each other.

A tailwind pushed us through the Cebolla Wilderness and its stands of pinon pine. Late afternoon brought us to El Malpais ("the bad country") National Monument, a striking, 114,000-acre ridge of solidified lava flows, ice caves, Zuni sandstone cliffs and La Ventana ("the window"), a natural arch carved in ancient sand dunes by wind and water.

Late in the day, after 72 miles, we reached Grants, population 9000. More than a century ago, Grants had been a railroad town where track for the Santa Fe Railroad was laid to connect the

Isleta Pueblo in New Mexico to Needles, California. A boom or bust town based on railroading, logging, ranching and mining, Grants was the uranium capitol of the world in the 1960s. Now its largest employer was Walmart.

After a rest day, we cycled onto Route 66, the legendary road west for the Joad family in *The Grapes of Wrath*. The road took us through Grants past old motels (one or two people for $19.95), the Roaring 20s Liquor Store (long closed) and the Uranium Café (between Lead and Silver Avenues). Nostalgia gave way to golden arches at the Interstate 40 interchange where Mel, daydreaming to Jerry Lee Lewis on his headphones, took a tumble. His chain fell off. He discovered three broken spokes on his rear wheel. His rear brakes stopped working. He pedaled onward.

Two hours later, after passing a state prison and entering Cibola National Forest, Mel's rear wheel was wobbling badly. He and Barney tried to adjust the spokes (we didn't carry spares) to "true" the wheel while I tried flagging down a driver to take Mel to Cuba, our destination the next night. By the time a lady stopped and agreed to help, Mel and Barney had straightened the wheel just enough to sort of work. Mel declined the ride and wobbled on, a little less badly.

Our road passed near Chaco Canyon National Historical Park, a complex of ruins sometimes called the "Stonehenge of the West." Those ruins provided the highest documented level of civilization reached by the Anasazis or other Native Americans north of Mexico more than a thousand years ago. Our gravel road, now in Navajo country, wound through dry washes and arroyos etched with hoodoos, mammoth rock formations that looked like sand castles and profiles of old men.

The Navajo people were exceptionally friendly and kind to us. They readily let us camp for the night in front of their Pueblo Pintado ("painted village") Navajo Nation Chapter House. Some of their sixty residents here were heading eight miles down the road to attend the Full Gospel Revival. We were tempted, but not enough. After 67 miles for the day, we went to bed wondering whether (a) Mel's bike would make 53 more miles into Cuba, and (b) if it did, whether anyone there could fix it.

We awakened and starting bicycling the road to Cuba, traveling through an arid landscape featuring mesas and arroyos. The wind came head on. We saw no one in the stark, remote area until we reached pavement a few miles outside Cuba, where litter analysis indicated the town had a McDonald's (yes; it opened three days ago), maybe a Wendy's (no), and Budweiser (Regular and Lite) was the king of beers here.

Cuba, population 760, was established by Spain in 1769 for its colonizing families. It had grown into a Wild West town that still had some shady (and shaky) characters roaming its streets. No one in town could fix Mel's bike. We learned that Espanola, which was off our route, was the nearest town that might have a bike shop.

We devised a plan. The next day, Mel would ride 62 paved miles to Abiquiu, which was on our route, while Barney and I would ride the rough, dirt course, taking two days to get there. The second day, Mel would go twenty miles off course into Espanola, hopefully get his bicycle fixed, and return to Abiquiu to meet us. With that settled, we dined at the excellent El Bruno's Ristorante y Cantina and spent the rest of the night dealing with their hot sauce.

The next morning we went our separate ways. Barney and I climbed into the Santa Fe National Forest, refilling our bottles at Horseshoe Springs, the only known water source for the day. Ten miles flew by in three hours as the air thinned and vegetation thickened. A pin holding Barney's trailer to his bicycle broke. Duct tape to the rescue.

The dirt road rose sharply. While I crept forward, riding in my lowest gear, Barney, pushing his bike, walked past me. Early afternoon brought dark clouds that threatened but spared us as we rode rough roads through a lovely forest filled with quaking aspens, various pines and firs.

After 37 tough miles, we pushed our bicycles a mile up an unridable pile of rocks called a road and camped in a 9200-foot meadow near an empty stock tank. If we hadn't needed the calories, we'd have gone straight to bed without supper. *Good night Mel, wherever you are. And good luck.*

The wind howled all night and into the morning, but relented as we ascended four miles on a rocky road that gradually became ridable. Barney's gps unit confirmed we had reached 10,000 feet and weren't totally lost. We rode at our own paces—classic tortoise and hare. Barney, riding strongly, was the hare while I caught him during his breaks. At high altitude, we literally sucked air while our red blood cells searched the air in our lungs to capture oxygen.

A succession of awful, butt-bouncing "roads" took us downhill. On Polvadera Mesa in the Jemez Mountains, we met a ranger who told us that many bears were in the area. We acted like we knew that, but made a mental note to start hanging our food in bags at night.

We left the pinon-juniper ambience of the Santa Fe National Forest to descend into Abiquiu. In the mid-1700s, soldiers had been dispatched there from Santa Fe to stamp out the practice of witchcraft. Eight practitioners had been sentenced to become servants to prominent Spanish colonizers. Perhaps it was the magic and light in the air that later attracted Georgia O'Keeffe, the famous artist, to make her home here.

We took a room at the Abiquiu Inn and met Mel, who told us his story. Yesterday he had ridden to Abiquiu as planned. This morning, he had waited all of thirty seconds at the edge of town before hitching a ride into Espanola. There the driver advised him to stay near his bicycle at all times since that town—known for its heroin consumption—had more than its fair share of questionable characters.

Many people in Espanola are poor; they rely on wood to cook food and to keep warm. Other residents, however, have money and commute daily to nearby Los Alamos to work at the National Laboratory, site of the Manhattan Project that developed the atomic bombs that ended World War II.

In Espanola, Mel found Randy, the bike person, sipping coffee at a local café. Randy had a thriving business. Many of his customers, he explained, were people who didn't have a car or weren't allowed to drive because of drug and alcohol problems.

Randy worked for more than an hour on Mel's bike. He took three spokes from another wheel, put them on Mel's wheel, "trued" the wheel, fixed his brakes, put a new, heavy duty inner tube in the front tire (which had gone flat), and adjusted the derailleur so Mel could use his granny gear without the chain slipping. The total bill was $10. Then Randy insisted on driving Mel the twenty miles back to Abiquiu.

We're back in business.

Late afternoon, I walked alone a mile into Abiquiu's tiny village square. In the center, atop red clay, lay the roofless remnant of an adobe building. A lovely sandstone Catholic church with stained glass windows graced one side. Its gate was open, so I walked to the front door, which also was open. When I stepped inside, cool air brought instant relief from the heat. I sat in a pew and silently meditated for a few minutes. Refreshed, I walked out of the church and village square and back to our motel without seeing a single person.

The next morning, we began the second half of our trip with our bicycles and bodies in good shape. My only ailments came from too much time in the saddle and sun. *Yes, Mother, I know I should wear sunscreen and a helmet.*

We pedaled through the Carson National Forest and into El Rito, a charming town of clay, stucco and sandstone buildings. Mel said it felt like we were in a different country, one where a major occupation seems to be driving around town in old cars with modern sound systems turned way up. The village housed several artist studios and Northern New Mexico Community College, which once was the Spanish-American Normal College, established in 1909.

We arrived before the tiny El Farolito restaurant opened, so we loitered for an hour, hoping to get lucky. No luck. Nobody was sure exactly when the restaurant opened. Barney finally declared he was moving on, and we followed. Our road was rutted from vehicle and bicycle tires, evidence of the quagmire created when water soaks into its clay.

Afternoon skies brought dark clouds but few raindrops. Time passed agreeably as we discussed recent Supreme Court decisions, Martha Stewart, diversity and our country converting to the metric system. We cycled through Vallecitos, population 200, which must be the ugliest town in America. Each "dwelling" and lot was a self-contained junk yard, complete with rusting cars on cinder blocks, car parts, trash, garbage and wild dogs. *I wouldn't go near this place at night.*

After 42 miles, we plunked down along Forest Road 42, near water dribbling from a culvert, and stared into the starry New Mexico night.

During the night, headlights from two pickup trucks bore down directly on me until the road curved them fifteen feet away from my tent. We broke camp at 8000 feet, the *low* point (in altitude) for the rest of our trip. Although we began with a climb, as usual, we confirmed that there are no bad miles before 10 a.m., and no good ones after 4 p.m.

We swept along a lush, green meadow. The arid lands of southern and central New Mexico lay in our wake, and northern New Mexico surprised us with verdant fields and thick forests. Burned Mountain (10,192 feet) preceded Cisneros Park, a vast panorama where deer and antelope played against a backdrop of the southern Colorado Rockies, which we would soon reach. The high country showed off its grasses and wildflowers, mostly of the purple persuasion.

In ten minutes, we squandered two hours of uphill work as we blasted five miles downhill on our only pavement of the day, reaching speeds of 40 mph on loaded bicycles. Then back to climbing.

Late afternoon, we crossed the Rio San Antonio—a trickle of water—and found a workable place to camp after 36 tough miles. As we went to sleep, Mel discovered a broken spoke in his rear wheel that affected his alignment. *The saga continues.*

I awakened at 5:30 a.m. and saw my breath. My left knee ached and yesterday's sunburn bit my back. My tent on a patch of weeds was surrounded by cow pies and some of their indifferent owners. Breakfast was a couple packets of oatmeal in water from this sad excuse for a river that plugged my filter last night. I put on the same stinky clothes I had worn for two straight weeks. *What am I doing here? Oh yeah, I forgot; I'm having the time of my life riding the Great Divide.*

We had to keep company all day with Forest Road 87, a miserable, gravel washboard. Conversation was sparse. "Are we having fun yet" passed as clever repartee. At the top of a climb I looked at my watch to see how much of the day was behind us. It was 8:24 a.m. *So much for the idea that there are no bad miles before 10 a.m.*

But Barney and Mel, with their usual good spirits, gradually lifted me out of my funk as we pedaled a succession of short, steep hills in the Cruces Basin Wilderness at 9000 feet. Since our bicycles go downhill about five times faster than they climb, you can do the math to figure out that we spent most of our time going up. Mel lost his granny gear again, but at least he was the most capable of us to ride without it.

Feeling weak and lethargic, I asked Barney and Mel to ride behind me, letting me set (limit) the pace. After lots of water, salt and sugar slipped down my throat, things improved. At the top of a steep climb, I stopped and waited for them. And waited. An hour passed. Puzzled, I walked back down the hill, confirmed I was on course, but saw no one. *What to do? Are they lost, or hurt, or broken down? Did they pass me without us seeing each other? Did they take a short cut I don't know about?*

I rode back down the hill and finally met Mel coming my way. He didn't know where Barney was, and he had already ridden back once to look for him. We rode back farther, checking every junction for tire tracks heading off course. Finally, way back, we found Barney, on course and under a tree working on his bicycle.

Barney explained that the threads of his rear axle (specially designed to pull his trailer) were stripped, and he'd been working for two hours trying to rig a solution. We spent another ninety minutes working on it, to no avail. Finally, we duct taped the arms of his trailer to a thick piece of wood we wedged onto the rear rack of his bicycle. Rube Goldberg would be proud. Barney still couldn't ride his bike-trailer combination because his bicycle sat loosely on its rear axle. But at least Barney could push it.

At 4:30 p.m., deep in the woods, miles from anywhere, Barney asked Mel and me to ride ahead to try to find help while he walked his bike, or, in the remote chance of a vehicle passing by, hitched a ride.

We left Barney and rode the steep, rocky road along beautiful 10,900-foot Brazos Ridge. Some sections were too rough to ride. Mel spoke in Spanish with a Basque shepherd, the only person we'd met all day, who told us we might get help a few miles down the road from the driver of a white pickup truck. On we went. No pickup appeared. Mel, now without rear brakes, squeezed his front brakes on descents and dragged his feet, giving new meaning to "brake shoes."

The sun set as we crossed into Colorado and reached pavement and the Rendezvous Steakhouse and Saloon. A cook told us Redneck Jimmy, who lived in a nearby cabin, might be able to help. When we found Jimmy and told him the situation and what we were doing, he asked: "Are you freakin' maniacs?" Mel and I looked at each other, our tongues tied.

Jimmy was low on gas. Since the only gasoline station was twenty miles away and closed for the night, we couldn't help

Barney until tomorrow. Defeated for now, Mel and I set up our tents in the dark on a patch of gravel and thought about Barney, back in the New Mexico night, walking his disabled system, with no help on the way.

We awoke at 5:30 a.m., saw our breath, cooked breakfast on the porch of the Rendezvous Steakhouse and Saloon, which wouldn't open for eleven hours, and waited until seven to knock on Jimmy's door. Jimmy and I drove to Chalma to fill up his gas tank and then drove in to look for Barney. Meanwhile, Mel and Gene, a nearby cabin owner, rode toward Barney on Gene's four-wheeler.

We met Barney after just three miles, near the narrow gauge tracks of the Cumbres Toltec Scenic Railroad, a historic route that once linked mining camps in the area. He explained that he had pushed his bicycle until midnight, taking a lengthy wrong turn in the dark, threw his sleeping bag on a tarp for a few hours of rest, and then resumed walking. He was in good spirits. *He is one tough man.*

We drove him to Jimmy's cabin and tried to figure out how to fix his bicycle and trailer. Using Jimmy's expertise—he was in the construction business—and supply of bolts, nuts and washers, the trailer arms were securely fastened low on the rear rack of Barney's bicycle (patent pending). Since the trailer no longer connected to the axle, Barney's bicycle no longer needed a special axle. So Mel persuaded Gene to kindly sell the rear axle from his mountain bike to put on Barney's bike. The solution worked.

Early afternoon we resumed riding. We pedaled up 10,200-foot La Mangas Pass, coasted down the other side, and then climbed upstream along the lovely Conejo River to reach a private campground, where for a change we camped near other people. After last night's challenges, we were very grateful to be together in good physical and mechanical shape. *Bring on Colorado.*

The next morning our tents wore a thin coat of ice. Barney moved stiffly, showing the effects of his ordeal. Mr. Sun gradually warmed the tree-lined valley in the South San Juan Wilderness as the Conejo River tumbled down its rocky bed alongside us. We passed people fly fishing and reached Platoro, which marked the completion of two (of the three) maps, and 715 miles, for this trip.

After breakfast, we lazed outside the Skyline Lodge for a couple of hours while Barney did laundry, proving (again) that his sanitary standards were higher than Mel's and mine. Meanwhile, I grabbed a very used copy of *Slaughterhouse Five* to read and watched a van from Amarillo, Texas pull up, advertising "Dog Spa: Self-Service Dog Wash." I pictured a poodle on a conveyor belt passing through a sudsy shower surrounded by whirling brushes, followed by an optional hot wax.

When we resumed riding, we discussed why we all prefer having our bicycles on our right side when we mount or push them. Barney is left-handed while Mel and I are right, so that didn't seem to be the reason. Mel wondered whether it was related to what he had read is the reason horses almost always run counterclockwise around tracks (as do humans): the way a horse fetus typically lies in the womb gives its spine a slight curvature that makes going counterclockwise easier.

Snow patches decorated nearby mountains as we churned up 10,500-foot Stunner Pass under a cloudy sky. Along colorful, mineral-rich mountains, the road plunged into a gorge, crossing the Alamosa River and several creeks. Water, water everywhere, but not a drop to drink. We knew these waters carried cyanide and heavy metal ions from long-ago mining operations, and neither our filters nor iodine could detoxify them.

What comes down must go up. Mel called the resulting, seven-mile crawl an "enjoyable climb," an oxymoron in my book. Four-wheelers buzzed by, one portly driver puffing a big cigar. Near the top, we met a hiker trying to find his pick-up crew. We hadn't passed them, so we continued on our route and soon found them. One was Gary, a veteran mountain biker, who tinkered with Mel's bike and invited him to his house to finish the job the next day when we arrived in Del Norte.

We found a gorgeous, secluded camping spot at 11,600-foot Schinzel Flats in the Rio Grande National Forest. A huge, panoramic view of alpine meadows, snow-dappled mountains and trees—we're near timber line—made this as pretty a campsite as we'd enjoyed on our entire Great Divide Ride and brought an excellent day to a fitting end.

You would think that sleeping in a tent more than two miles above sea level would be cold. Not that night. An early morning breeze chased away the night blanket of clouds, leaving a clear, calm, balmy morning.

We descended into Summitville (strange as that sounds), an EPA Superfund Site. There a huge mountain, scarred from gold and copper mining, was being chewed up and trucked to a mill to extract its ore, while vegetation was being planted to reclaim the land. Mel and I ambled through old shacks of the ghost town left from 700 miners who had lived there a century ago in what was then Colorado's highest incorporated town. The water was colorful, contaminated and undrinkable.

We climbed up to Indiana Pass, at 11,910 feet the highest point of the entire Great Divide Ride. Our reward was a 3000-foot plunge out of the Rio Grande National Forest into Del Norte, a town of 1700 people. There the main grocery store doors were covered with "I'm Proud To Be An American" while the Baptist Church reader board on Main Street proclaimed "God Bless The USA."

A few miles from town, Mel got a flat tire—number 4 if you're counting. The special, strong inner tube he had gotten from Randy back in Espanola had ruptured. We put in another tube so Mel could make it into town, where he found Gary (who we had met yesterday) to fix Mel's three broken spokes, wobbly wheel, balky derailleur and rear brakes. *Mel's bike has been through more hands than Madonna.*

We took a motel room, cleaned up and rested. Two-plus weeks of riding at altitude had taken a toll. Despite a nearby restaurant, we discovered we couldn't eat two real meals in one day; we were too used to nibbling all day long. Indeed, we would discover, once the trip ended, that Mel had lost twelve pounds, I'd lost six, and Barney had lost an unknown number in addition to the nearly forty he shed before the ride.

At dawn, we cycled north from Del Norte, crossing the sparkling Rio Grande River and passing bushes loaded with currants that, Barney explained, "are good to charge your batteries." The map steered us through a maze of rough, intersecting, dirt roads, mostly unsigned. Mel was stylin' with a functional bicycle and green, wraparound sunglasses he had bought in town yesterday for $2.

Forest Road 41G led us out of the desert and up a canyon studded with 30-million-year-old volcanic rock formations of columnar basalt. We ascended 10,200-foot Carnero Pass in the Rio Grande National Forest as the afternoon darkened and winds swirled.

After five quick downhill miles, we pitched our tents near a stream and dove inside, waiting for the storm to strike. The gusts were impressive, but for the 20th straight day, no serious rain fell. Barney and Mel laughed and declined my offer to put their food in a bag I hung that no bear could reach unless it was taller than four feet or had a bear IQ above three.

We started the next day with an eye-watering, nose-dripping, finger-freezing descent in early morning shade along a picturesque canyon. Then 21 miles of pavement replaced a slightly longer dirt route as we tried to gain time. A six-mile climb brought us across the Continental Divide at 10,100-foot Cochetopa Pass.

At the summit, we met a damsel in distress who was overheating (that is, *her SUV* was overheating). Her cell phone received no service there, nor did Barney's. We got her going with shrewd advice and mechanical know-how honed by years of experience: put water in the radiator and drive for help.

Outside Gunnison National Forest the landscape—valleys, hills, sagebrush, trees, rocks—looked perfect for cattle and cowboys, which suddenly materialized. Environmentalists capitalized on local patriotic fervor as signs declared, "Patriots Don't Litter." Mel stopped at a trailer that hot afternoon to ask for water and was turned down, presumably by a patriot.

We pedaled along Cochetopa Canyon and into Doyleville,

which consisted of two houses and fenced-in animals—notably white elk and black yaks. Briefly on pavement along a broad, treeless basin, we met a trio of fraternity brothers from Lamar College in Tennessee who were riding from Washington, D.C. to San Francisco to raise money for some worthy cause. They had identical bikes, shirts, shorts and shoes, but we liked them anyway. They were sponsored by a bike company. *Why didn't we think of that? We should have been sponsored by Frito-Lay, Hostess and Little Debbie.*

At the end of the pavement we reached Sargents, whose sign said, "Elevation High, Population Few." This town of 25 people had a convenience store, but the café was closed for repairs and no lodging or camping was available. We limped four more miles before camping by a pretty stream after an 11-hour, 69-mile day. *We'll celebrate when we have the energy.*

At dawn, Mel discovered that the shirt he had washed in the creek last night and hung on his tent to dry was frozen solid. In fact, frost encrusted all our tents. But cold was our friend as we began a twelve-mile climb back into the Gunnison National Forest. On our left was Marshall Creek, transformed into a series of slow-flowing pools by hundreds of beaver dams. Aspens surrendered to pines atop 10,800-foot Marshall Pass, which crossed both the Continental Divide hiking trail and the 469-mile Colorado Trail that connected Durango to Denver.

The descent brought us to a solo biker riding the Great Divide Ride and then two women riding a nine-day section. After 39 miles, we reached Salida, an attractive town of 4700 people at the headwaters of the Arkansas River. Here you can hire a fly fishing guide or rent kayaks, rafts, Jeeps, bicycles or four-wheelers. We treated ourselves to a motel room and explored the old section of town, complete with fine homes and good eating places. The clear day showed off several of Colorado's 14,000-foot peaks looming over this town we all liked.

Mel visited the bicycle shop to get another set of hands on his bicycle and was advised to throw away his rear wheel when he gets home. The bike man then asked Mel his age (63) and whether he really thought he could pedal the 2800-foot climb tomorrow. Little did he know that two other 60-year-olds would be joining Mel.

In the morning, we exited Salida and climbed through junipers, pinon and granite into the San Isabel National Forest. Mel and I rested in the shade while Barney, with mathematical precision, rode twenty meters farther into the sun to reach his exact odometer setting for a break. If he rode off a cliff, Barney would stop on the way down if he reached his preset distance for a rest break.

After four hours and twelve miles, we topped out at 10,200 feet. Gleaming in the sunlight were many 14,000-foot peaks of the Sawatch Range, including the Collegiate Peaks—Harvard, Yale and Princeton. Mel felt weak as we pedaled through a massive meadow ablaze with purple, orange and yellow wildflowers that soon gave way to an almost dry basin, and then rangeland.

Mel gradually regained his mojo as he soldiered on. We reached a grader working on the road surface, softening it. In the long run, the grading would be beneficial, but the immediate effect was, in Barney's words, to "make a bad road worse."

We met a couple from Vermont cycling the Great Divide. They asked about Salida, which riders had voted their favorite town on the entire ride. (Whitefish, Montana ranked second.) Then we met a man from Adventure Cycling, the company that had devised and mapped the ride we were doing. He was going to take seventy people on a catered ride the next week, so he was driving this section of the course to check it out. Fascinated by the way Barney's trailer was now fastened to the bicycle's rear rack (thanks to Redneck Jimmy), he took pictures and notes.

Twelve hours and 48 miles brought us into Hartsel, population 110. Seeking a place to camp, we walked by the restored schoolhouse and into the tiny library, startling the only people there—an elderly couple engrossed in computer games. No luck there.

Elsewhere in town, we talked with Violet and Ron, who kindly let us camp in the weeds behind their café and saloon. Instead of a babbling brook, our company that night consisted of barking dogs, pickup trucks, honky-tonk music and babbling bar patrons. Our tents proudly stood beside a dumpster overflowing with waste grease.

Violet opened her café at 7 a.m. After eating her spicy Mexican meal last night, I didn't dare order her breakfast burrito. Water in the area is rich in iron and sulfur, so after breakfast we bought drinkable water and were on our way.

We cycled 25 miles across optimistically-named South Park (not the TV show), arid rangeland actively being developed by realtors. Dozens of roads intersected ours, each with an attractive street sign and most without a single house.

As we rode through the broad basin, snow-capped mountains of the Continental Divide followed along our left (western) flank and then curved across our northerly route. We had crossed the Divide a total of 26 times, and our final crossing, the next day, lay straight ahead.

Como, population 45, provided a welcome lunch at the historic (Train) Depot Café. We climbed, under cloud cover, to our final campsite at 10,400 feet just south of Boreas Pass. A sign said our road would be closed in a week for construction, so we had arrived just in time. At sunset, we camped alone atop pine needles listening to fine music from Selkirk Gulch Creek.

We awakened to our final day. It was exciting to know we

were going to finish, but I knew I'd miss the daily challenges, adventures and company. Once we reached Silverthorne, Barney and Mel would drive off with family members while I'd board a bus bound for Ellensburg.

We broke camp for the last time, our routines honed to high efficiency. The sky revealed we would make all 25 days without significant rain. We'd been lucky, to be sure, but the timing and direction of our trip had maximized our chances of getting lucky.

In the crisp morning air, we ascended the snow-capped mountains with legs and lungs toughened by nearly a month of riding. Snow melt trickled down the road. We slipped between the mountains at 11,500-foot Boreas Pass. On top sat a beautifully restored Section House, originally for the Colorado and Southern Railroad, which had been converted into a visitor center and winter ski hut.

We coasted ten miles down the mountain ridge into Breckenridge, the famous ski area. Mel basked in the sun, sipping a latte, while Barney scouted ahead for the sixteen-mile bikeway into Silverthorne. The mountains were magnificent in the azure, cloudless sky—a perfect ending to our journey.

We left Breckenridge along the Blue River on a bicycle path filled with hundreds of bikers—steely-eyed grandmas pumping their pedals, a couple on a tandem recumbent, children with their parents, serious bikers in garish outfits. Mel discovered three more broken spokes—a total of nine for the trip if you're counting—as we cruised together the final miles, passing through Frisco and into Silverthorne.

The Great Divide Ride was complete—2469 miles total, and 1033 on this trip. Since we began in 1999, you could say the journey took us four years, or two decades, or two centuries, or two millennia.

We finished and celebrated at the same motel where, last year, I was laid low by a Giardia infection. As we prepared to go our separate ways, I asked Barney and Mel whether they were stronger or weaker than the day we began our adventure. Both said they were stronger.

"And you're a lot stronger," Barney said, looking at me and smiling, "so stay downwind."

12 CHASING A GHOST

Bicycling began to replace running for my summertime fun. But the rest of the year was prime time for running. I loved running in the cooler months as I approached age 60. In February, at age 59, I had run the Rocky Raccoon 100-mile trail run in Texas in the fast time of 19 hours and chump change.

It went to my head. I looked up ultrarunning track records for my approaching age group (60-64) and saw the name Carlton Mendell, who had set records for 100 km, 100 miles, 200 km and 24 hours, all in one remarkable run in Brunswick, Maine nearly two decades earlier. Ephraim Romesberg held the record for 12 hours.

I didn't know Carlton Mendell, and didn't know if he was still alive. I could have used the Internet to find out, I suppose, but I liked keeping him mysterious because of what he did to me, at least in my mind.

Can I catch a little late lightning a few months after I turn 60? I registered for Across the Years (ATY), a run near Phoenix, Arizona that begins on December 29, 30 or 31 and ends the morning of New Year's Day. The time you start depends on which event you are running: 24 hours, 48 hours, or 72 hours. If you're still running at midnight on New Year's Eve, you get to celebrate with fireworks and champagne.

I registered for the 24-hour event and trained hard. ATY would be my best effort in years, with no excuses. Carlton Mendell became a ghost that haunted me for months as I trained to chase his records. I calculated the pace needed to break each one, and wondered whether it was realistic to try running that fast and far.

Three weeks before ATY, snow fell in Ellensburg and tendonitis kept me from training. Carlton whispered in my ear: "Remember, no excuses."

Eighteen years earlier was the only other time I had chased a record: the U.S. 24-hour track record for my particular age, 42. The year before, I had run what I then thought was 100 miles at Western States, on mountain trails, in a touch over 20 hours, so the single-age record of 116 miles in 24 hours on a flat track seemed possible. I had never done a long track run, however, and didn't know that one month after the run, I would be diagnosed with cancer.

I entered the No Bullshit 24-Hour Run in Ventura, California, flew to Los Angeles, and grabbed a night bus to Ventura. Connie, the race director, kindly met me at the station and took me to her house to get some sleep. Sometime during the night, another runner, Bob van Deusen from Oregon, climbed aboard another bare mattress in her attic.

The next morning, Connie kindly gave us breakfast, piled all the race paraphernalia plus Bob and me into her car, and drove to the track, all the while talking about being slowly poisoned by mercury leaching out of her tooth fillings. Unlike Bob, I was a rookie at 24-hour track runs, so she peppered me with advice on how to run.

The track was old and cindered. A few runners set up tents along the track to house their clothing and extra food and drink to supplement what the race provided. Bob and I just piled our supplies together on a tarp. As the starting time neared, Connie called the thirty or so runners together, explained we would be getting coverage later from a Japanese-speaking TV station in Los Angeles, and performed a Buddhist kata to protect and guide us during the next 24 hours.

My plan was to run, for as long as I could, 23 minutes at a comfortable pace, followed by one lap at a faster pace (to change my muscle action), and then leisurely walk a lap while eating and drinking. After one hour, when several of us had exceeded six miles, Connie scolded us about going out too fast.

Twelve hours later, I was maintaining that pace and in the

lead. As night deepened, Bob sat down on our tarp to change clothes. When he returned to the track, he was sporting a yellow tail, which turned out to be the squashed remains of a banana. Later, I stopped at our tarp to get a slice of pizza left over from the night before. I discovered it was unusually flat and had acquired a banana flavor.

With aching muscles and blistering feet, I gradually slowed and then was reduced to just walking. Finally, after 22-plus hours and one lap over 130 miles, I hoisted the white flag, retired from the track, and sought medical help for my blisters. The volunteers took one look and declared they wouldn't touch them.

The television crew arrived from Los Angeles and talked with Connie, who quickly renamed our event the "Ventura" 24-Hour Run. When they asked who was winning, with more than an hour of racing remaining, Connie pointed to a guy lying on a massage table along the track and said he had already won.

I opened my eyes to a smiling, somewhat confused Japanese man extending a microphone in my direction and asking me about the race. With memories of mountain runs vaguely penetrating the thick fog in my skull, I didn't help much: "I liked the course. It didn't have any steep hills, rocks or snakes; it was well marked; and I didn't get lost." He nodded, smiled, and backed away uncertainly.

Tired, stinky and on blistered feet, I had to get home in time to teach my 8 a.m. class the next day. Hobbling through the Los Angeles airport, wincing with every step and trying to get to the gate in time to catch my flight to Seattle, I saw a little old lady come up to me and kindly ask: "Can I help you with your bag?"

I instinctively replied, "Thank you, but I'm fine."

We both know I'm lying.

But I felt fine, back at the track in Phoenix, ready to chase Carlton Mendell and his records. As our 9 a.m. start neared, I pictured him sliding next to me and wishing me luck. We watched other runners, in various states of fatigue, continuing their 48- or 72-hour runs. I pointed out Jeff Hagen, a friend who had regularly run more than 200 miles in 48 hours and was trying to set yet another U.S. age group (55-59) record in that event.

Jeff would achieve his goal, going 214 miles. His main competition for the overall 48-hour win was Mark Heinemann, a member of Divine Madness (DM), a communal group led by charismatic Marc "Yo" Tizer, a philosopher-coach who believed ultrarunning is a way to attain enlightenment. His disciples worked at subsistence jobs and pooled their money. Tizer set the rules, regulated training and diet, and regularly had alcoholic parties at which monogamy was discouraged.

DM had several runners there, in various events, plus a support crew operating out of a large infield tent filled with food, cooking equipment and boxes of running shoes. By the time the 48-hour race ended, Mark and Jeff would become good friends, despite their rivalry, and Mark would become the overall winner with 222 miles.

Little did Carlton, Jeff and I know that Mark would soon become a ghost. At next year's ATY, Mark would again run more than 200 miles in the 48-hour event, but he would look like he was struggling the entire time. Twenty-five hours after that run ended, his body would be found alone in his hotel room by DM members. An autopsy would reveal his cause of death: bacterial double pneumonia.

As we watched Jeff and Mark circle the track, waiting for our race to begin, Carlton said he'd never tried running for 48 hours. He asked me if I ever had, so I told him about the one and only time I had tried, at ATY many years earlier.

I had come to Phoenix intending to run for 24 hours at ATY. When I drove to the home of the race director to register, he told me the 24-hour race was full. But he still had space in the 48-hour event. Did I want to try that one? I shrugged and said "Okay." *Why not?*

I arrived at the track early and walked into the bathroom, waking Ray Krolewicz and his son who had driven from South Carolina and spent the night sleeping on the concrete floor. The race began with Ray, wearing jeans, sprinting around the track for several laps, leaving us all in his wake, before abruptly slowing down.

When I stopped to get a piece of clothing from my tarp along the track straightaway, I walked at an angle from the track to the tarp, got my gear, and then angled back to the track. Ray, a veteran who had won more ultramarathons than anyone I knew, sternly warned me that the official rules say I must return to the track at exactly the same place I leave it when I go to my tarp. I thought about the rule, debating its logic, but complied.

During the night, a police car, lights flashing, arrived at the far end of the track. Two friends, runners who had come to the track together, had gotten into an argument that had escalated into fisticuffs. One of them was bleeding and had called 9-1-1. The officer told them to be nice and drove away.

Three times during that night I had crawled into my rental car, reclined the seat, and turned the engine and heater on to catch 45-minute naps. I was trying to pace myself; 48 hours was unknown territory, both for sleep and distance. After the first 24 hours, and a bit over 100 miles, I was in the lead. But I could see trouble ahead as another runner, a veteran of six-day runs, wasn't far behind and looked pretty fresh.

That year, Harold Sieglaff, who founded ATY, in a fit of social conscience had hired homeless people to count our laps.

Whenever one of their assigned runners completed a lap, their job was to record the time and total number of laps on a piece of paper formatted for that purpose. Early in the second 24-hour period, Harold introduced me to Jim, a relaxed fellow, who was my new lap counter.

Each time around the track, I made eye and voice contact with Jim to make sure he counted my lap. He would smile and nod at me. After a while, getting quite tired, I asked Jim what my total distance was so far. When he told me the same distance— 129 miles—I'd had three hours earlier, I was stunned. And defeated. After checking with others, and learning that no one had been recording my laps all that time, I took my wounded pride, spent body, and blistered feet off the track, vowing never again to attempt running for 48 hours.

I'd kept that vow, but now was ready to take on Carlton and his records. The time for talking was over. We stood together at a high school track where the weather was good and the aid station we passed every lap carried everything we could want. *No excuses in sight.*

I tied onto my shoe a chip. After every lap, I'd cross a mat where that chip would be detected, confirmed by a beep I could hear, and a computer would maintain a continuous record of how many laps I had run. *No offense, Jim, but I like this system better.*

I'd done the calculations. My plan was to run ten-minute miles, and then die as slowly as possible. We began running. Early in the race, I enjoyed the camaraderie of other runners circling the track, but in my mind the Flamingos were crooning "I Only Have Eyes for You" as I focused on Carlton.

We ran the first hour together, and the second, and the third. Alongside the track, I had my special food and drink. I stopped occasionally to refuel, walked short stretches, and kept my eyes glued to my watch while doing mental arithmetic.

I was working hard, but Carlton just seemed to float along. After eight hours, he had moved several laps ahead. If I wanted his 100-km record, it was now or never. I chased him for two hours, knowing the extra effort would hurt my 24-hour performance, and finally caught him. I pulled slightly ahead, knowing his record was frozen in time, and reached 100 km five minutes before he did.

I walked and jogged a few minutes, enjoying the record and trying to come back to life. I didn't have much energy left. Then I remembered the 12-hour mark. That one would be close, too. In a fog of fatigue, I ran as hard as I dared for the next 80 minutes. When the clock struck 12 hours, I had another record.

I walked around the track, hoping my energy would magically return. It didn't. Carlton relentlessly held his pace, cutting into my lead. He passed me an hour later, this time for good. I knew my run was over. The next time he went past me I shook his hand, thanked him for challenging me to run with him, and acknowledged he was still the 100-mile, 200-km, and 24-hour champion.

With a slight grin, he offered me a rematch any time, any place. Then he disappeared down the track and into the night while I slipped into the weary bliss of motionlessness.

13 GREAT DIVIDE RIDE CANADA

Soon after Mel, Barney and I completed the Great Divide Ride from the Canadian to the Mexican border, Adventure Cycling mapped a new, 240-mile extension of that route, going from Banff, Alberta to the Canadian-Montana border.

Two years later, Mel and I decided to scratch that itch and ride the new section. Barney couldn't join us, but three local friends decided to get in on the fun. One was Tim Englund, an accomplished ultrarunner and chair of our university's Mathematics Department who in his younger days had led church youth groups cycling across the U.S. The second was Ethan Bergman, a triathlete who would later, as President of the Academy of Nutrition and Dietetics (formerly the American Dietetic Association), carry the Olympic Torch in England a few days before the 2012 Olympic Games began. Our third newbie, Pat McLaughlin, was a historian and university librarian who was possibly our best all-around athlete though his longest run was "only" 100 km; the rest of us had completed 100-mile runs.

We five drove in two vehicles to Eureka, Montana, ten miles south of the Canadian border at Roosville, and camped in a city park, sharing space with a grizzled old guy from Alaska who apparently had traveled here by bicycle to prospect for gold.

With Barney, we had always awakened by 6 a.m. and started riding by 7, but without him, I figured we'd have a more leisurely schedule. The next morning, a driving rain storm pounded my tent and woke me up. I looked at my watch—6 a.m.—and the ghost of Barney appeared.

I crawled outside to see clear skies. *What's going on?* Sprinklers had erupted all around us in the park, drenching our tents. We quickly pulled up stakes, dragged our tents to dry ground, and loaded five bicycles, five sets of soaked camping gear and five no-longer-sleepy bodies into Pat's pickup truck to drive to Banff. Ethan's car would stay in Eureka until we finished our ride.

We threw down breakfast in Eureka. Afterwards, when we jammed three heavily caffeinated bodies into the front seat, somebody's knee jabbed a gear or button or something. The truck was stuck in "Park" and wouldn't move. *How many people does it take to figure out how to shift a Toyota truck?* Fifteen minutes and one review of the owner's manual solved the mystery.

We drove to the border crossing, where a Canadian official peered dubiously inside the truck and asked: "How many of you are in there?"

"Five."

"And how many seat belts?"

"Five," we (rep)lied in unison.

Perhaps we misunderstood; maybe he was referring to firearms when he next asked: "Are you carrying personal protection?"

We looked at each other, puzzled. Finally Tim responded: "We don't have any condoms."

The official rolled his eyes and waved us into Canada, unprotected, without checking anyone's ID.

We reached the entrance into Banff National Park. Pat's explanation of our intentions there was so long and convoluted that the official waved us through without collecting the entrance fee. After five cramped hours, we reached Banff, where we discovered we couldn't park Pat's truck unless we bought a season pass for $125; even then, we could only park for 72 hours in one place, after which the vehicle would be towed.

What to do? Since we needed to leave the truck five to seven days, we were instructed to buy the pass and then work out arrangements to park the truck at the majestic Banff Springs Hotel, built in 1888. The hotel clerk there told us it would cost another $150. Pat blinked his baby blues, his eyes beginning to moisten, and stammered that we'd been planning this trip for a year and already were getting low on money. The clerk smiled sympathetically and silently slipped him a free parking permit for one week at the hotel.

We saddled up and started riding at 4 p.m. on the Spray River Trail behind the hotel. In minutes, we left civilization and entered lush woods, prime grizzly bear territory. Mel soon ground to a halt with a flat tire. We repaired it and moved on. After nearly four hours and twenty miles, climbing up to 5500 feet on Goat Creek Trail, we camped beside the crystal clear waters of Spray Lakes Reservoir.

A nearby camper, whose family of six was in one large tent, told us that sites were $20, so we clipped that bill to the post bearing our camp number. I tried tossing a rope for a bear bag that got hopelessly entangled in branches and couldn't be pulled back down. But Tim's rope worked. The ranger drove by, saw our $20, and informed us that it was $20 for the first tent and $18 for each additional tent. Since we each had a small tent, the bill for five came to $92. Seeing our shocked looks, he settled for $50.

We awakened to a beautiful, lightly-clouded morning with a refreshing bite in the air and watched two mule deer stroll through camp. After a leisurely breakfast of oatmeal and coffee, we filtered water from the reservoir and began riding at 8:30 a.m., cruising along the lake on a picturesque trail free of motorized vehicles.

I mentioned that in the last 2000 miles of the Great Divide Ride I hadn't had a flat tire. You guessed it: three minutes later, I had a flat tire. We skirted Spray Lakes Reservoir for twelve lovely miles and rode across Canyon Dam. Thirty yards ahead of us, a large brown bear shot across our trail, perhaps startled by bells tinkling atop Ethan's and Tim's bicycles.

Steep trails, water crossings, and blown-down trees tested, and sometimes bested, our technical skills. The Canadian Rockies provided a magnificent backdrop as Mel repaired another flat tire. Tim, Ethan and Pat, our strongest riders, led the way while Mel and I tried to keep them in sight. This became the pattern for the entire trip.

The clouds thickened and darkened. The final five miles of our 40-mile, eight-hour ride in the Peter Lougheed Provincial Park climbed to 6000 feet. We were tired. Balking at another $92 camp site (or a group site for $250), we found an, er, undisclosed location deep in the woods at an excellent price. Tim stunned himself and us by successfully tossing a long rope over part of a power line pole so we could hang possibly the world's highest bear bag. Another bear precaution was to walk some distance from out tents before cooking and eating our evening meals. Our camp stove cuisine left nearly everything to be desired. Raindrops chased us into our tents for a chilly night.

We knew the start of the next day's ride would be tough. The map describes where we would have to push our heavily-loaded bikes up "a virtual wall." After an hour of sweat, and a grand total of three miles grinding up a little-used service road under power lines, we were calling for our mommies.

We reached the summit of Elk Pass, at 6440 feet the highest point of our ride. We dismounted and sat, gingerly and sideways, in the soft grass as part of our Butt Restoration Project. Here we were both crossing the Continental Divide and entering British Columbia from Alberta.

We mounted our bikes and charged down the steep, faint road. I don't want to call that road bumpy, but on the ride down Pat dislodged his panniers three times, Mel lost screws to both his bike rack and bike pump, and my sleeping bag bounced off. Only Tim and Ethan escaped unscathed.

At the base of the descent, we rode into Elk Lakes Provincial Park, a shining, subalpine string of mountain faces, cold lakes and remnant ice fields. We reached a little-traveled gravel road and pedaled along a wilderness corridor and the Elk River, spotting birds, two deer, a moose and squirrels (males and females according to Ethan, who apparently has excellent eyesight).

Each day we tried to reach 20 miles per hour at least once. On this roller-coaster road I exceeded 20 mph twenty times. Each time the moment of truth arrived when, going down a steep gravel road, I released my brakes. The sudden acceleration, almost a free-fall, left me breathless and knowing that any bad surface ahead could cause me to lose control and adorn my body with terminal road rash.

After fifty miles, we reached Elkford, a town of 3000 people and an oasis. There we discovered a community campground with showers, our first in three days. Afterwards, we actually approached people without them running away. Mel and Ethan nursed a few brews in a nearby pub and learned from Solomon, a Fijian who had moved here thirty years earlier, that coal mining was the main industry in the area.

The next morning, Tim awakened to a (lack of) caffeine headache, which he treated vigorously with coffee. Thanks to ear plugs, Pat had his first good night of sleep. We broke camp, climbed 800 feet, and meandered past coal mines shooting smoke plumes straight up into the windless, cloudless sky. Mid-morning we lazed on a bridge over the Fording River, dotted with fly fishing folks. The river kept agreeable company with us for fifteen miles.

Mel noticed that his only footwear, a pair of sandals that clipped into his bicycle pedals, was falling apart. Duct tape to the rescue. Earlier in the day, we had heard about the Canadian Duct Tape Bandit, who held up banks with his face (except for his lips and one eye) covered with the stuff.

Our map was off by five miles, but we stayed on course. We passed a murder of crows. *(I learned that word from Tim, and you can look it up in the dictionary if you don't believe me.)* Suddenly we met two bikers. One, from Japan, had been riding for eighteen months. The other, from Switzerland, had started at Prudhoe Bay, Alaska before meeting the Japanese rider, who had persuaded him to cycle a ways with him. When they separated, a few days later, the Swiss rider would continue pedaling to the southern tip of South America.

The final twenty miles of the day on hot pavement brought us into Fernie, a skiing and fly fishing Mecca of 4000 people, described on a local T-shirt as "a quaint little drinking town with a mountain biking problem." We found a campground in town, bought bicycle supplies, and enjoyed the best meal of our trip at the Curry Bowl. After dinner, we ambled around, enjoying the ambience of this fine town.

The night was a vivid reminder of the urban camping experience: trucks continuously rumbling through; trains blowing their whistles every hour; a young man in a tent twenty feet away talking loudly, well past midnight, about how a girl at the wedding said he was the cutest guy there. Only Pat, with his ear plugs, slept well. As we awakened, a nearby, massive motor home disgorged three poodles to overrun our tiny site. *They're just darling.*

Things got better. We packed up, and were soon sitting outside a coffee house at 8 a.m. on Fernie's main street, sipping our brews of choice. Tim exclaimed: "This is fabulous. You get up, ride and go to bed. Everything you need is on your bike. You stop and enjoy whenever you want to. I could live like this."

We pedaled past a big ski hill and followed the Elk River downstream on a good gravel road flanked by poplars and conifers. In the lead, Tim startled a still-spotted fawn. Near Elko, the lead riders (Ethan, Pat and Tim) met a black bear on the road. As Pat reached for his camera, the bear scampered away, obviously camera shy. At Elko, we stopped for lunch at the main business establishment, a convenience store that featured live bait, chain saws and massive amounts of fireworks.

As we ate, Ethan learned, via cell phone, that unexpected company was arriving, so he needed to get home right away. We changed plans on the fly and charged for the border. Our new plan was to ride the remaining seventy miles today; then, very early the next morning, Ethan and Pat would drive in Ethan's car from Eureka, Montana back up to Banff, retrieve Pat's truck, return to Eureka, and then drive us all 400 more miles back to Ellensburg.

We pedaled in earnest. On one steep, paved downhill section outside Elko, we reached 40 mph as vehicles blasted past. We passed barns, meadows and ponderosa pines like they were standing still. Nearby we spotted Lake Koocanusa, a 90-mile pond spanning the border that had formed upstream from a dam, completed in 1975, across the Kootenai River near Libby, Montana. The lake's name was apparently devised by a committee trying to please everyone. (You can figure it out by taking each three-letter section of the name and making a wild guess where it came from.)

We crossed the border without incident and cycled the final ten miles into Eureka. Fighting a stiff headwind on a highway with no shoulder, I looked up and saw a car coming straight at me, passing another car in a no-passing lane. The driver, a young man with one arm crooked around a young woman, looked straight at me and smiled as I had to ride into the ditch.

We found the same park in Eureka where we had camped before, this time being careful to set up our tents a respectful distance from all water sprinklers. Mel, who had bought a large bottle of duty-free champagne at the border crossing, iced it in his pannier when we reached Eureka. Then we drained it. I don't remember what happened after that.

14 LEADVILLE REDUX

When we rode the Canadian section of the Great Divide Ride, Tim Englund extracted a promise from me, one I would keep. When he had moved to Ellensburg several years earlier to become a math professor, he had started running with our group at noon and on week-ends. His hard work and physical skills turned him into an excellent ultrarunner, so after a few years, he decided to run the Grand Slam of ultrarunning.

The Grand Slam was born in 1986, when Tom Green of Maryland ran all four of the oldest 100-mile trail runs: Old Dominion (in Virginia), Western States (California), Leadville (Colorado) and Wasatch Front (Utah). The next year, two people completed the Grand Slam, and the idea grew in popularity.

Eventually the Grand Slam was formalized: runners would apply and pay for the attempt, and those who succeeded would receive an Eagle trophy. By the time Tim applied, the Vermont 100 had replaced Old Dominion, narrowing the window of time between the first (Western States) and last (Wasatch Front) to eleven weeks. I'd run all those races, but never in the same summer.

Tim knew that fewer than half of the thirty or so runners who started the Grand Slam each year completed it. Many faltered at Western States, for a variety of reasons: being the first race, it eliminated those who weren't in good enough shape, were injured, or who couldn't handle the early season heat. Of the remaining three, Leadville took the heaviest toll. Not only did it present the challenge of high altitude, but its tight cut-off and finishing time limits disqualified the most runners.

Because he feared Leadville the most, Tim asked me to promise that if he finished the first two (Western States and Vermont), I would come with him to run Leadville, "The Race across the Sky," eighteen years after my first time there.

Tim had first seen Western States when he had paced me for my fourth (and final) time there. The first three trips had gotten me 24-hour belt buckles, but the fourth time was not the charm. I wasn't in good enough shape that year and was suffering when I met him at Foresthill (62 miles), where pacing could begin. We had stayed together for several long hours, mostly walking, until I surrendered at the river crossing. He hadn't told me he was hurting, too; only later did he learn he was pacing me while enduring a stress fracture in his leg.

A bachelor, Tim said he had learned much from that

experience. Most importantly, he had discovered that Foresthill, where many people were waiting to start pacing their runners, was a great place to meet fit, unattached women. He had also learned how many personal relationships were ruined while crewing or running Badwater, a 135-mile race in Death Valley in July.

The year of his Grand Slam, Tim finished Western States and Vermont in fast times and reminded me of my promise. So in August we jumped into his Subaru Outback and headed for Colorado. Late night brought us to a nondescript truck stop somewhere in Utah. He pulled over to the edge of a parking area and crawled into the back of his car to sleep while I slipped, under cover of darkness, into the small tent I put up alongside his car.

When we were driving the next day, Tim's fuel light came on. The nearest gas station was 70 miles away. "Don't worry," he said. "The warning light is set up to be idiot-proof." He proved it an hour later when we refueled and the pump reading matched the tank capacity listed in his car owner's manual.

Late afternoon, climbing to two-mile-high Leadville, we passed remnants of the Climax Mine, which in its heydays had produced half of the world's molybdenum. When it had closed, 25 years earlier, the mine had laid off more employees than Leadville now had people.

We arrived, in pouring rain, two weeks early so we could

acclimatize before the race. The second week we had reservations, but we were on our own for the first several days. In town, we spotted a soggy sheet of paper advertising an all-you-can-eat spaghetti dinner up the street for some worthy cause. After the meal, we asked locals where we could camp. One recommended a place near the garbage dump a mile northeast of town. "It's free," he explained, "and the cops won't bother you there."

Who could resist? Not us. We drove to the dump and, not surprisingly, had the place to ourselves. Tim went to sleep in his car while I put up my tent in the rain, crawled in, and had sweet dreams fueled by aromas I'd never met before.

The next morning, I laid out my dripping tent on shrubs and ducked into the car with Tim. *Time to start showing him the course.* We parked in town and rode our mountain bikes out and back along the first thirteen miles of the race course, dodging rocks, skirting campers, and enjoying views of Turquoise Lake. Tim's technical skills and pace left me behind. He finished first and waited patiently in his car while the rains returned and I wandered around town trying to figure out where we had parked.

After another soggy night at the dump, Tim woke up to a headache and nausea. *Welcome to high altitude.* After a latte, we drove out to explore the next ten miles of the course—the first big climb of the race. We hiked the rocky trail up to Sugarloaf

Pass. On top at 11,071 feet, we gasped for breath and then ran down. The three-hour adventure left us listless and light-headed.

By the next day, Tim's nausea and headache were gone. We drove to a secluded spot along Half Moon Creek and set up camp in a place that actually smelled good. *Time to explore the second main hill on the course.* We mountain biked a few miles to the Colorado Trail and hid our bikes in the bushes. After a big climb and three-hour run on the next section of the course, we capped the day with a sun shower, camp-stove supper, and a quiet night far from anyone else.

An ad in the Leadville newspaper by Cloud City Medical said: "Suffering from high altitude sickness? Don't let it ruin your stay. Oxygen delivered to your door." It reminded us that on race day, oxygen canisters would be delivered to the aid station atop 12,600-foot Hope Pass, the third major hill, to help suffering runners.

We moved to a real campground where my Golden Age Passport got us a 50% discount. An older man in a nearby motor home talked about his Golden Age Passport, which he had bought at a ranger station when he turned 62. The passport was good for life and provided free entry into national parks in addition to camping discounts. He said the pass saved him $250 last year alone, and its price—$10—was ridiculous. "The government should charge at least $50," he added.

We took a day off. Sort of. We joined a friend, parked at 11,300 feet and hiked up to 13,400-foot Mosquito Pass on the highest jeep road in the country, enjoying the 360-degree vistas on top.

We spent two more days exploring the course, including a round trip up Hope Pass. Afterwards, as dark clouds covered the Pass, we thought about the facts that (a) late afternoon thunderstorms were common here, and (b) more people died from lightning in Colorado than in any other state.

In camp, Tim talked with a man fine-tuning his bicycle. He was there to ride the Leadville 100-Mile Mountain Bike Race in a couple of days. That race, which later attracted such riders as Lance Armstrong and Levi Leipheimer, used a lottery to select about 1000 riders each year.

This man rode semiprofessionally. Tim asked him about the illegal use of drugs in the sport, referring to problems in the Tour de France. "Everyone cheats," he replied. "They have to in order to compete. The ones that get caught are the ones whose doctors screw up."

We broke camp and checked into the Leadville Hostel, our home for the next week, which was swarming with runners. Food, drink and war stories abounded, all under the genial management of Bill, the owner, who must once have been a flower child. He cooked mounds of food each morning and evening and offered meals at moderate prices. We were on the honor system: if you ate, you just kept track of the meals and paid him when you checked out.

Tim got in the spirit of things and volunteered to help direct traffic for the mountain bike race, so I did the same. Our job was to stand in the rain for four hours at the 95-mile checkpoint, making sure the riders turned right. We watched some very tired bikers; some injured, and some with injured bicycles. But all were courteous, thanked us, and kept going. We vowed to be sure to thank the wonderful volunteers when they helped us the next week. Clearly affected by the shortage of oxygen, Tim started thinking about doing both the 100-mile run and bicycle events the next year.

As race day approached, we vegetated. Our spirits and weights rose. We visited friends who had just arrived. Joe Dana was trying to become the second ever 70-year-old finisher here. He made and sold gaiters—sleeves that fit over the tops of running shoes and extend above stockings to keep out trail debris. He had prodded his (and our) friend Eb Engelmann, age 64, to come along. Eb's ticket to finishing would be to keep making good time late in the run when he was mostly walking, which he did very well.

The day of reckoning arrived, and the 4 a.m. gun sent 389 runners into the darkness. Tim disappeared up ahead; we wouldn't see each other until twelve hours later. My climb up Sugarloaf Pass seemed much harder than it had been eighteen years ago. *This hill has grown.*

Things didn't improve on the second hill. I was near the back of the pack, and by the time I descended into Twin Lakes at 40 miles, I felt like I was moving in slow motion. My watch confirmed that I was. The third climb, up Hope(less) Pass, was harder yet. I was spent when I reached the top in deteriorating weather. There I watched hail sting a nearby runner, bent over and vomiting, while two other runners shivered in the aid station surrounded by llamas that had brought up oxygen and other supplies. But the scenery—what I could see of it—was magnificent.

As I descended the back side of the pass, hail turned into rain and the trail turned into mud. Partway down, I met Tim. He was miles ahead of me and coming back up after reaching the 50-mile turnaround point. He was wet, muddy, and moving slowly. In short, he looked bad. We stopped briefly and talked. I tried to encourage him and wished him well as we went our separate ways.

But my run was over. I had nothing left when I reached the 50-mile aid station at Winfield. I arrived shortly before the cut-off time, but knew I had no chance of making it back over Hope Pass in time to beat the next cut-off time. Kenny Rogers sang in my ear: "You've got to know when to fold 'em."

I surrendered. It wasn't a hard decision. A volunteer cut and removed the bracelet on my wrist, officially making me a DNF (Did Not Finish).

An older couple, crewing for another runner, kindly gave me a ride back to the Twin Lakes aid station so I could check on Tim. She was 69 years old and he was 76. They wore T-shirts they had earned the week before when they had won their age groups in the 14-mile trail race to the top of Pike's Peak. When I told them my 40th wedding anniversary was the next day, she said: "Your wife will be glad to get you back safe and humble."

When they dropped me off at Twin Lakes, mile 60, I was glad to learn that Tim had already arrived and continued on. At the aid station, I watched a runner, who had been on the course for seventeen hours, stand up too quickly from his chair and pass out, falling and hitting his head on something hard. As he lay on the concrete floor, a medic checked him out. Ten minutes later, he headed out into the cold, rainy night with his headlamp on, ready to climb 1400 feet, determined to finish the last 40 miles.

I hitched a ride back to the Hostel and was fast asleep when Tim arrived, smiling. He explained that his energy had returned and he had finished comfortably; in fact, no one had passed him during the final 40 miles. He said the low point of his run was when he saw me on Hope Pass. I wasn't sure I liked how that sounded, but I gave him a high-five anyway.

Late in the run, he added, something did go wrong with his vision; maybe his contact lenses were blocking oxygen from entering his eyes. Whatever the reason, he could hardly see when he finished. But, except for possible strep throat, he now felt fine. He also told me that Joe hadn't finished, but Eb had.

Three weeks later, on the most difficult of the four courses (but with a generous time limit), Tim finished the Wasatch Front 100-mile run near Salt Lake City. His cumulative time for the four races made him the fastest of the eleven men who completed the Grand Slam that year. But the lone woman to complete the Slam, Darcy Africa of Colorado, was even faster.

15 GRAND CANYON

Ever since I had sat around a campfire at White River Campground on my run around Mt. Rainier on the Wonderland Trail, listening to Susan Gimbel talk about her runs back and forth across the Grand Canyon, I'd wanted to do that run. But other things kept popping up on my "to do" list.

If distance runners had an official bucket list, one entry, near the top, would say "Grand Canyon." It wouldn't be a race, of course, since races aren't allowed in national parks, but it's hard to resist running in one of the Seven Natural Wonders of the World, a place explorer John Wesley Powell called "the most sublime spectacle in nature."

With my biological clock ticking, I decided it was time to scratch that itch. When I mentioned it to Tim Englund, I discovered he had the same itch. Better yet, when we mentioned the idea to several running friends, they couldn't resist, either. So we huddled to figure out the details.

We all wanted to do a double crossing: running from the South Rim to the North Rim and back (or the reverse). Both directions, of course, have the same distances and options for trails. Most runners start at the South Rim since it is more developed to accommodate visitors.

Up and down the North Rim, you use the North Kaibab Trail. Up and down the South Rim, however, you could use either the Bright Angel Trail or the South Kaibab Trail. Using the first means a round trip of 46 miles; the second makes the round trip about five miles shorter. There are only two hills, but they are doozies. You climb and descend 4500 feet dealing with the South Rim (at 6900 feet); the North Rim (at 8200 feet) gives climbs and descents of 5800 feet.

Another decision was when to do our run. Summer was out because it was just too hot. In winter and early spring we'd face snow and ice at high elevations, and some water sources would be turned off. Autumn, though, seemed just right. Because we all had day jobs and limited vacation time, we picked Veteran's Day weekend in early November.

We made reservations at Bright Angel Lodge, right where that trail begins, so we decided to run on Bright Angel Trail both directions. South Kaibab Trail, our other option, was several miles away. It could be reached from our lodge by regular shuttle bus service during the tourist season, but not in November and not late at night, when we expected to finish.

So the Friday before Veteran's Day, our band of eight—three

women and five men—flew to Las Vegas or Phoenix and drove to the South Rim, arriving late. We passed through the unstaffed national park entrance and muddled around in the dark until we found Bright Angel Lodge. The receptionist, partially awake, gave us room keys. Before we crashed into bed, we loaded our running packs for the next day and agreed to meet in the lobby at 6 a.m., ready to run.

Our alarms erupted. We stumbled out of bed, downed some food in our rooms, and headed for the lobby. The place was totally empty, except for the receptionist, as we filtered in, snapped a few pictures, and walked out into the cool darkness. It was hard to believe, after thinking about it for so long, that the time had come to run the Grand Canyon Rim-to-Rim-to-Rim (aka R2R2R). *Wow. We really are going to do this.*

Briefly on cement, we turned on our flashlights and headlamps, jogged past the Kolb Studio, found the trail, and headed down. The surface is rough, with many deep ruts. It was hard to get in a rhythm negotiating all the steps and stones installed to prevent erosion. Every few strides brought another switchback. We constantly saw and smelled mule excrement from the beasts that carry tourists and supplies up and down the canyon. *All part of the adventure.*

I found myself in the lead, more limiting than setting the pace. We passed petroglyphs carved in rocks but couldn't see them in the dark. Neither could we see the steep drop-off on our left, which was just as well. But we certainly knew it was there.

Suddenly, from behind me, came a sharp cry of pain. One of our runners, Diane Jones, was down. She had twisted her ankle, and it was swelling rapidly. Although she was the only one in our group who hadn't run the distance we were doing today, Diane had run 50 km (31.1 miles) and was very tough. Indeed, several years later, she would have to fight back after being hit by a car suddenly turning into her while she was bicycling. Multiple surgeries later, she would work very hard and regain both her running and bicycling fitness.

Diane was in pain, but she didn't dare take her shoe off to check the damage because she knew she wouldn't get it back on. She stood up, gritted her teeth, and said, "Let's go." So we did.

Near dawn, after 4.6 miles and 3000 feet of descent, we reached Indian Garden, an oasis in the rocky landscape. There Havasupai Indians used to grow squash, corn and beans near Garden Creek. Several deer meandered among the cottonwood trees near a stone cabin bearing a wooden roof. Water was available somewhere nearby, but we didn't stop to look for it since we were carrying enough to last several more hours.

Bright Angel Trail followed a natural break in the southern cliffs and was originally used by Havasupai Indians to link the South Rim to Indian Garden. Later, prospectors had used it and extended the trail down to the Colorado River. In 1928, ownership had been transferred to the National Park Service, which then built the South Kaibab Trail, giving tourists two routes between the South Rim and the river.

Just past Indian Garden was a junction that offered a side trip (three miles round trip) to Plateau Point, a popular vantage and turnaround point for tourists making a one-day round trip on mules from the South Rim. We followed the main trail, running through a gully of water-sculpted stone. As the sun rose, the slope began to flatten.

Sandstone gave way to dark gray schist that had formed 1.75 billion years ago. A few backpackers appeared, hiking out from the canyon. Near the bottom, on a ledge along the Colorado River, we met people coming our way on horses and mules. They told us we had to go around them on the outside, along a serious drop-off.

Our downhill running ended as a sandy trail took us to the silver suspension bridge spanning the Colorado River, where many tourists enjoyed multiday rafting expeditions. There I couldn't help but think about a woman who had run the same trail one summer and run out of water. She had climbed down the cliffs to get water from the river. Her body was found on those cliffs.

All eight of us planned to make the complete round trip except Steve Varga, who had a herniated disk. An accomplished runner—he had finished the Vermont 100-mile race in less than nineteen hours—he planned to turn around soon, probably at Phantom Ranch. But he was managing his pain for now and kept going.

After crossing the river, we began to climb. For several miles the grade was gentle, and we ran as much as we comfortably could. We crossed another bridge and reached Phantom Ranch, a private place and popular tourist destination. You could arrange to ride a mule here from the South Rim, eat dinner, stay overnight in one of their cabins, and the next day have breakfast and ride back.

We entered their small canteen, the only place we could buy supplies. They had surprisingly little in stock, maybe because it was November. We bought coffee and lemonade. That was all. Outside, at picnic tables, we refilled our water bottles and took a break, gobbling down food from our packs. Speaking of gobblers, when I pulled out a three-year old PowerBar, a roaming turkey instantly filched it from my hand, and then nearly choked on it. *It serves him right, though he's probably doing me a favor.*

There we continued to get acquainted with Suzanne Weightman, a Pennsylvania runner who Steve had invited to join us. They had met at the Heartland 100-mile race in Kansas where they ran many miles together and finished together, with Suzanne winning the women's championship. She was the only one in our group not from Ellensburg, but she fit in seamlessly.

With 9.6 miles in the bank, we continued north from Phantom Ranch on the North Kaibab Trail as the grade gradually steepened. After eight cactus-filled miles, we found a pump, our last sure source of water until we reached the summit of the North Rim and returned here.

We filled our bottles and said good-bye to Steve, who headed back to the South Rim. Disappointed that his back wouldn't allow him to make the entire round trip, he would return a year later (after surgery) and fill in the missing piece: starting at the North Rim, descending to this pump, and then climbing back to the top.

As we seven ascended the North Rim, the scenery became even more spectacular. We saw very few people, but in the sunlight we spotted precipitous drop-offs on our right. They were disconcerting to several, especially Pat McLaughlin.

If we had a contest involving as many different sports as you could think of, Pat would win. But he would pass on mountain climbing because of his fear of heights. Here he was wearing special sunglasses—essentially blinders that blocked his peripheral vision. He kept going, eyes straight ahead, while declining Diane's ever-increasing bids to buy those glasses.

The climb steepened, and we did no more running until we reached the top. On the way up, we met two 20-something men, shirtless and carrying water bottles in their hands, moving at a startling clip. Later, we learned that one was Kyle Skaggs, who was setting a R2R2R record (since broken) of 7:37 using the South Kaibab route. He would finish in less than half the time we would take.

Pinon pines and junipers appeared as we ascended. Two miles from the summit, we happily discovered water at Supai Tunnel, so we topped off our bottles, enjoyed the red rocks, and climbed through the tunnel. Spirits were high, except mine. I became a zombie. The final two miles to the high point of the course was my low point. *Maybe the altitude.* Just below the summit, the others stopped at Coconino Overlook to take photos, while I silently trudged by.

On top of the North Rim, 23 miles from where we started, we enjoyed spectacular views and had a picnic near an alpine forest of Douglas fir, ponderosa pine, and aspens. Soon we were all shivering in the high, cool air. Time to go back.

As we descended, we gradually warmed up and breathed more easily. Past Supai Tunnel, we returned to the amazing section of trail blasted out of massive, vertical cliffs of 330-million-year-old Redwall limestone. The work to construct that trail boggled my mind, and a picture taken there still is my computer screen saver. The sheer drop-offs, now on our left, were still disconcerting, but the path was wide enough. *Just concentrate and don't do anything stupid.*

Lower in the canyon, we saw the river and the climb ahead up the South Rim. The colors and shadows were dazzling as the sun began to set. Visibility ebbed, as did our pace.

Near the bottom, Jody Scheffelmaier went through a low point. A slender Energizer Bunny and skier who finished first or second woman in her first three 50-km trail races and whose longest run was 53 miles, she was trying to quell a rebellion in her stomach. Nausea made her very quiet. We tried to help, but as Greta Garbo would say, she "vants to be alone."

Tim Englund, our strongest runner, came to her rescue. All day he had been a good shepherd, staying with those in back or anyone else who needed help. Now he convinced Jody to try a bland energy drink, hoping she'd be able to tolerate its (lack of) taste and get her energy back. Within an hour, she was feeling and moving well again.

With flashlights and headlamps turned on, we reached a bustling Phantom Ranch. Lights were on in the dining hall, where a group of tourists were enjoying a fine meal. Since meals were by reservation only, we stayed outside and retrieved food and drink we had stashed nearby on our way out. We jogged downhill in the dark, crossed a bridge and headed for the Colorado River.

Once across the river, we began our eight-mile climb back to the South Rim. The stars glittered in a beautiful night sky. Indeed, we'd had perfect running weather, with temperatures ranging from a little above freezing to a high of 65 degrees. What remained was mostly a long hike with invisible drop-offs.

Craig Carlson and I brought up the rear. On the switch-backing trail, we heard our friends' voices above chattering away, and we did some reminiscing of our own. An excellent age-group swimmer, Craig had completed many Ironman triathlons, including the Hawaii edition, in fast times.

We talked about his first 100-mile run, the Arkansas Traveler. When he had finished, in less than 24 hours, he was lying on a cot in the medical tent, receiving intravenously his first of two bags of saline solution, when I asked him to compare running 100 miles with doing an Ironman triathlon. He replied with words I've never heard him use, before or since. Then I reminded him that when we stepped into the airport to fly home after that run, he was immediately offered a wheelchair.

The final climb was long but steady. We enjoyed the peaceful night and just kept our mouths and feet moving. About 11 p.m., we reached Bright Angel Lodge and learned that Steve had arrived there four hours earlier. Time to shower and dive into bed.

The next morning, we ate breakfast together at a nearby restaurant, shared stories of our excellent adventure, and exchanged verbal high-fives. Now we knew, for the rest of our lives, that we had "run" the Grand Canyon Rim-to-Rim-to-Rim.

Our smiles widened when we strolled outside and traced the

route we had taken, spotting the opening in the north wall where our trail went. Then we read the warning sign we hadn't seen in the darkness of the previous morning when we began our adventure: "Do not attempt to hike to the river and back in one day."

16 ALASKA'S GOLDEN CIRCLE

Every summer, Dad would get the family car greased, filled with gasoline and fresh oil, and announce that we were going on a road trip. He and Mom would pile us four kids into the car and start driving. And driving. During the day, we would stop only to refuel, have a picnic lunch, or visit a historic place.

When I, or my siblings, had to pee, we didn't stop. Instead, we'd use a potty in the car. When the potty got full, Mom would fling its contents out the front passenger's side window on the fly, sometimes reminding us kids to first roll up the back window on her side. After a few years, we noticed a few rust spots developing on the back of the car on the passenger's side.

By the time I had finished high school, I had visited, however briefly, all of the lower 48 states. When I moved to Washington to begin teaching, I figured the last two states—Hawaii and Alaska—would be easy to collect. Hawaii was. But for 35 years, Alaska eluded me.

With cycling becoming my favorite summer activity, I checked the Internet to look for good bicycle rides in Alaska and discovered the Golden Circle, a 360-mile ride from Haines to Skagway. Though it begins and ends in Alaska, the route (more a triangle than a circle) also crosses a piece of northern British Columbia and part of the Yukon Territory.

I was sold. With visions of Alaska dancing in my head, I had no trouble persuading three of the usual suspects—Pat McLaughlin, Mel van Houten and Steve Varga—to join me for the adventure. We set a date, and each person figured out his best way to get to Haines, Alaska and back home from Skagway.

Pat, Mel and I boarded the Alaska Marine Highway ferry at Bellingham, Washington for the three-day trip to Haines There we would meet Steve, who would fly into Juneau and then take the ferry to Haines.

As we boarded the ferry, Mel sported a new bicycle that fit inside a suitcase. We crammed our bikes and gear into a nook on the ferry's car deck, filled our arms with necessities, climbed to the upper deck, and plopped our sleeping bags, mattress pads and food on easy chairs to claim our space. We chose a spot under a roof looking out the stern of the boat. Just in front were tents duct-taped to the uncovered deck. Forty people shared space on that deck (one of several).

Many passengers had booked cabins, but we were hardly roughing it. Our ferry had a snack bar, dining room, movie lounge, bar, hot showers, and covered sitting space. While Mel and I checked out the dining room for supper, Pat added hot water to his dehydrated meal and was pleasantly surprised by its taste, proving that it is good to keep expectations low. That night we slept on deck in the open air, warmed by ceiling heaters, until rain blew in under the roof and onto our sleeping bags at 3 a.m. We adjusted and snored on.

The next days brought thick clouds and morning mist. The Inland Passage showed off zillions of trees, thousands of inlets, hundreds of islands, dozens of sun breaks, and a few dolphins plus orca and humpback whales. For two 55-degree days we cruised smoothly, sometimes as close as 200 yards from shore.

With time on my hands, I browsed the paperbacks on board, picked up *To Kill a Mockingbird*, and started reading. By the time our bicycle trip would end, and I would board the ferry and return the book, I would say to myself: *I am so happy I never read this book in school. If I had read it then, I could never have appreciated what a rich, wonderful story it is.* And when I would see the movie, a month later, I would feel the same way.

After two nights we docked, along with four cruise ships, at Ketchikan, a town of 12,000 people that receives 160 inches of rain a year and has eight elementary schools. We walked two miles into town, where tourists swarmed souvenir and jewelry stores, snapping up wares made locally and in China at special, low prices (today only). We watched visitors fish in a creek teeming with salmon returning to spawn. When we posed for a photo at the base of a large totem, Mel spotted a man tossing his still-lit cigarette onto a bed of flowers. Seeing Mel retrieve the burning cylinder to dispose of it properly, the man explained: "It's a bad habit of mine."

Mel replied: "Yes, it is."

Our next ferry stops were at Wrangell, Petersburg and Juneau. In Wrangell, we walked off the ferry for an hour and met children sitting at card tables in the parking area with garnet stones for sale. A quarry owner there allows children to collect and sell rocks studded with small garnets to raise money for their school.

We bypassed Sitka, but would stop there on the return trip. I was anxious to visit Sitka Lutheran Church, established in 1840, when the country was under Russian control. In 1846, it housed the first pipe organ on the west coast of North America. My mother and stepfather had spent two happy summers greeting visitors to that church, with my mother, whose graduate degree is in organ performance, giving them short concerts on the famous organ.

After three fine days cruising north, our ferry stopped at the terminal five miles outside of Haines. We disembarked, packed all our gear (including Mel's bicycle suitcase) onto our bicycles, and pedaled into town. There we met Steve, who had arrived the day before and had spent the night at the same hostel where we would all sleep that night.

First settled by Tlingit Indians 6000-8000 years ago, the town of 2400 people was settled by whites in 1881 after a visit by the naturalist, John Muir. Surrounded by mountains, glaciers and water, its main industries are tourism, commercial fishing (especially all five species of Alaska salmon) and government.

The next morning we ate breakfast at the Bamboo Restaurant. More than a century earlier, this had been the Hotel de France, known for its French cuisine. The cuisine had changed, and we were served by the owner, who pointed to an old picture on the wall of her momma Teng, who had bought the business 56 years ago. She, like all the other people we'd met in town, was exceptionally friendly.

Clouds filled the sky and a few raindrops splattered our bicycles, each loaded with 25-30 pounds of food and gear, as we stepped out of the restaurant and looked for the Haines Highway, our route for the next three days. The highway was built by the U.S. Army in 1943 to transport war materials and soldiers and was named a National Scenic Highway in 2009. We found our road angling northwest, following a centuries-old Tlingit trading trail to the interior.

As we prepared to leave town, Mel and Steve discovered that

neither was carrying a spare inner tube. Pat's and my spare tubes had a different kind of valve and wouldn't fit their bikes. The next place to maybe buy a spare was 151 miles up the road, and the only store in Haines that might have tubes wasn't open yet. So off we went, fingers crossed.

The smooth road and tailwind took us 3000 feet up along the snowy St. Elias Mountains. We followed the glacial-fed Chilkat River, where several large fish wheels captured specimens for tagging, measurement and release. We pedaled past Chilkat Bald Eagle Preserve, home each Fall and Winter to more than 3000 national symbols, the largest such congregation in the world. We stopped, but were too early to see them.

Next came the 33 Mile Roadhouse, our only source of food and gas for 130 miles, open every day of the week except Tuesday. It was—you guessed it—Tuesday. We stopped briefly, shook our heads, and pondered what might have been.

After 41 miles, we entered British Columbia. The customs officer looked at Steve's passport and asked him where he was from. Tired and distracted, he replied: "I don't know." I pictured him being frog-marched away in handcuffs and turned over to U.S. Homeland Security. But the official was kind, and Steve rallied to answer the remaining questions without further incident.

When we left Alaska, the miles morphed into kilometers, a

unit embraced by everyone in the world except Americans and (last I checked) folks living in Liberia and Myanmar/Burma. *Only our powerful triumvirate of nations stands strong against the evil metric system that apparently is too hard for us to learn and too expensive to adopt.*

Mel and Steve led the charge up a tough climb as Pat, normally our strongest rider, suffered a power (calorie) outage. We stopped and cooked an early dinner, and then cycled a few more kilometers to our campsite. This was one of several tactics we used to reduce our risk of attracting bears, especially grizzlies.

After 54 miles, we perched tents alongside Three Guardsmen Lake. Besides us, not a single person (or even a married one) was in sight. We threw on DEET to discourage the mosquitoes (surprisingly active in the 45-degree breeze), hid our food away from camp, and called it a fine day.

We awakened, gobbled down instant oatmeal and coffee, and rode, immediately descending through a dense mist. Pat had his mojo back and led the way. At 3000 feet, the green, treeless, densely-bushed mountains were adorned with enough purple and gold wildflowers to gladden the heart of any University of Washington Husky fan. Traffic was light and litter almost nonexistent.

We skirted the Tatshenshini-Alsek Provincial Wilderness Park. After an hour, we enjoyed brief baths of sunlight, our first glimpses of sol in two days. The scenery was magnificent as the tailwind pushed us on. Mel, who has biked all over the world and run a marathon on all seven continents, declared: "This is as good as it gets."

We entered the Yukon and rode along the eastern boundary of Kluane National Park, featuring mountains, lakes, open vistas and the largest nonpolar alpine ice field in the world. After cresting 3500-foot Chilkat Pass, the highest point on our trip, we plunged down to Million Dollar Falls Campground, which we had heard was closed due to excessive bear activity.

Hardly anyone was around, but the campground looked open. We claimed sites, hiked to the falls, filtered water, and enjoyed down time on a breezy, partly cloudy afternoon. During supper in camp (a secure distance from our tents), Mel's iPod, complete with speakers, serenaded us with oldies, transporting us back fifty years.

Morning brought frost, but no bears. Up a hill and down through a fog layer. Pat led all day, making it look easy. Mountains flanked us to the west, leaving the eastern side for lush terrain, most impressively Dezadeash Lake.

A porcupine crossed the road in front of Steve, stopped, stiffened, aimed, but didn't fire. I saw occasional scat, but no scatters. A dirt road exiting into the autumnal First Nations Klukshu Village revealed about twenty buildings, signs to the gift shop, and a place to hear stories from elders, but nary a soul.

Back on course, sixteen miles of bad road waiting to be paved tickled our tailbones, but otherwise we enjoyed a smooth, sunny, 65-degree, tailwind, eye-candy day. We camped at Haines Junction, population 900, where tomorrow we would turn onto the Alaska (ALCAN) Highway. We pitched our tents and embraced the twin pleasures of showers and real meals. 151 miles down and 209 to go.

Built in 1942 to connect the lower 48 states to Alaska, the Alaska Highway would take us, in the next two days, 100 miles east to Whitehorse. On that road, the next morning, we noticed terrain flatter and drier than along the Haines Highway. Our new road also featured scrub spruce, sandy soil, evidence of forest fires, and much more traffic and litter.

We met two biking couples. One, from Portland, Oregon, was riding to Argentina and quickly passed by. The second, from Vancouver, B.C., pedaled with us for five hours, telling us about their three-week ride, including "The Top of the World" route from Dawson City to Tok, Alaska. In two previous years, they had biked around Cuba, and from Mexico to Chile. Neither wanted to look another Snickers bar in the face for a very long time.

The scenery beneath a ribbed canopy of clouds was pleasant, but didn't compare with the first three days. After twenty miles, we stopped at a gas station, guzzled a Coke, and asked the attendant how far it was to the next place we could buy a Coke. He replied: "Whitehorse," 80 miles down the road.

Late in the day, we set up camp and hung bear bags in woods behind the Takhini Burn rest area. Like other rest areas, this one consisted of two pit toilets, a picnic table, and a bear-proof trash container. No running water.

Steve, our rookie tour rider, wanted me to pass on to you his five pieces of advice (which I've mercifully shortened): (1) make lemons into lemonade; (2) let your friends make the mistakes first, and learn from them; (3) if you've had surgery for prostate cancer and experience "leakage," Maxipads work; (4) use dirty socks for wash cloths; and (5) wear wet clothes in your sleeping bag at night to dry them out.

Most importantly, remember that Steve, Pat, Mel and I are much better at giving advice than taking it. I might add that no one else I've ever met thinks number (5) is a good idea.

Day five was Groundhog Day. We spotted the critter and its shadow as the temperature began climbing toward 85 degrees. Another day pedaling east on the Alaska Highway with the same scenery, following the Yukon Plateau but with more climbs and dips (besides the four of us) than yesterday. Cottonwoods and various evergreens lined the road as we crossed, and filtered water from, the Takhini River (Tagish Indian for "mosquito river"). Pat, his usual sunny self, zoomed ahead while I rode shotgun.

Besides the groundhog (or was it a prairie dog?), our total collection of wildlife sightings for the day consisted of four wild horses and two elk. Unfortunately, the elk were painted on road signs.

Late afternoon, we cycled into Whitehorse, population 23,000 and capital of the Yukon Territory. This city, linked to Skagway during the Klondike gold rush a century ago and connected to other areas by river and highway, is a major transportation hub. We camped along the mighty Yukon River at the very scenic Robert Service Campground, named for the "Bard of the Yukon," whose most famous poem is "The Cremation of Sam McGee."

We dined with our two riding friends from yesterday (Alvaro and Jacqueline) to recharge our fuel tanks for the final two, harder riding days. Thanks to showers, the patrons didn't flee to distant tables when we strode into the pub.

The next morning we began pedaling the same ol' Alaska Highway, with the same ol' scenery and the same ol' massive motor homes towing SUVs, leaving their carbon Bigfootprints all over the Yukon. After ten miles, parting was such sweet sorrow (not) as we turned onto the South Klondike Highway, completed in 1979, that would lead us 100 miles southwest into Skagway, our final resting place.

The improvement in scenery and serenity was instant except

for the jarring sight of a thoroughly wrecked car on one side of the road and a less wrecked (but just as dead) moose on the other. (Full disclosure: only Pat saw the moose; the rest of us blissfully cycled past it, staring at the wrecked car.)

As we pedaled, the greens got greener and the mountains whitened. Nearing the small village of Carcross, we looked for the Cinnamon Cache Bakery, known (according to our 12-year-old guide book) for its fine coffee and cinnamon buns. Not finding it, we kissed our buns good-bye.

Two young bikers from Berlin at the end of their three-week trip stopped to chat. Tomorrow they would fly from Whitehorse to Frankfurt, Germany. In two previous, longer trips they had pedaled from Anchorage to Phoenix, and from New York City to San Francisco.

Steve's rental bike suddenly couldn't shift into its third (high) gear, so Mel used his magic fingers to try to fix it. Soon Steve couldn't use first gear, either. Eventually, he could sort of use all three gears, so Mel declared he could work for Fred at our local bicycle shop as we all silently rolled our eyes.

A tough afternoon climb took the starch out of us. The scenery was beautiful, but after 300 miles, insufficient calories, and now a headwind, the miles were hard-earned. We finally spotted a road down to Windy Arm, Tagish Lake that led to a picture-perfect spot on a sandy beach, our prettiest campsite of the trip. We skinny-dipped in the cold lake as a gentle breeze refreshed, and a bald eagle perched atop a nearby tree while the sun set in the cloudless sky.

A couple of young boys walked by, looking for a cap one of them had lost. A few minutes later, their mother and another woman stopped by and talked. After they left, Steve, coming from somewhere, declared, "They are prostitutes."

Pat pondered why his bicycle computer had suddenly switched to kilometers, and Steve wondered why his cell phone photos were all upside down, when Bert, a nearby camper, invited us over to his beach spot for a nightcap. A lifelong resident, he explained that we were camping at the headwaters of the Yukon River, which eventually emptied into the Bering Sea.

Over glasses of wine, Bert said not to tell anyone (so you didn't hear this from me), but Yukon winters aren't so tough anymore. "They used to include a couple weeks at -40 degrees," he said, "but now they rarely get much below zero (Fahrenheit)." *It's a good thing Robert Service's famous poem about Sam McGee freezing to death was written back in 1907, long before global warming arrived.*

Dawn of our last day brought a sense of urgency as last night's gentle breeze strengthened. The prevailing south wind, so welcome the first three days of our trip as we pedaled north, now impeded our ride to Skagway. Pat and I had to cycle those 55 miles fast enough to catch the afternoon ferry back to Bellingham, or wait one week to catch the next ferry. (In two days, Mel and Steve would fly out from Juneau, so they weren't under the same time gun.)

As we were packing up to leave camp, we discovered our bear bag stubbornly snagged in a tree. Six-foot 5-inch Mel, on tiptoe atop my bicycle seat, just barely reached and freed the bag.

Steve left first. We rode solo; every man for himself. I saw no one except when Pat powered by, his strong legs churning higher gears than the rest of us could manage. Since we all lived in Ellensburg, home to several wind farms, we were used to fighting headwinds, which today varied from benign to fierce.

But we were far from home as we looked at the scenery, the most majestic of our trip. I thought of Norwegian fjords as I stared at the succession of lakes to the east lying against mountains whose north faces bore wrinkles of snow. To the west, sparkling creeks cascaded down another ridge of coastal mountains. Frequent signs said: "Avalanche Area: Do Not Stop."

Skagway, a town of 900 people, awaited us. First occupied by Tlingits and settled by whites in 1897, it became the first incorporated city in Alaska three years later. The White Pass and Yukon Route, a narrow gauge railroad line built more than a century ago, took Klondike gold rush miners from Skagway up over White Pass to Whitehorse. We heard that one condition for cruise ships agreeing to stop at Skagway had been to restore the train ride up the mountain as a tourist attraction. The town had complied, buying back railroad cars that had been sold and moved to Colombia, South America.

The town receives a million visitors each year, 90 percent from the nearly 500 cruise ship stops. The ship companies own many of the stores in town—especially those selling jewelry.

By late morning, tour buses and rental vehicles filled the road, a sure sign that the cruise ships had docked. Sixteen miles from Skagway, we made the final, wrist-numbing, backbreaking, butt-burning, hyperventilating ascent of 3300-foot White Pass. Our reward was a screaming, brake-smoking, gulping plummet into town, reaching speeds of 40 miles per hour without pedaling a stroke, passing cars, and interrupted only by a 40-minute wait to clear U.S. customs.

We made it—360 miles in seven days and still friends. We found each other in town, celebrated at a coffee house, and said good-bye until we would meet again in Ellensburg. Mel and Steve grabbed a campground, while Pat and I boarded the ferry and looked forward to three days of sheer laziness while our body parts recovered and we savored some excellent memories.

17 BITTERSWEET

In his early 50s, he asked me to help pace him in a 100-mile trail run, his first in seven years. He had run a few shorter ultras during those years, but he didn't have much time to train. His family and work came first.

Seven years can be a long time, especially when, for the last two years, he had been living with a diagnosis of Parkinson's disease. That diagnosis is difficult and uncertain, especially in the early stages, and his symptoms were mild. But my brother has Parkinson's, so I recognized my friend's slightly slower speech and movements.

I'm not going to tell you his name because I don't want news of his medical condition to hurt him professionally. My brother lost his long-time job just one month after he was diagnosed, a coincidence according to his employer. I've learned from my brother that Parkinson's is really a galaxy of diseases, each with its particular set of symptoms and treatment options.

I was with my friend, many years ago, when he started ultrarunning. He brought joy and youthful exuberance to our group as we got to see running through his fresh, new eyes. We had run together in his first ultra, 100 km. We shared the lead until midway, when he left me and won the race, setting a new course record and breaking mine.

I'd run with him when he won a 24-hour race, and when he won a 100-mile trail run. During the trail run we had met when I was going out on one piece of the course and he was returning. We stopped and talked. He was in the lead, but he had wanted to spend a couple of minutes taking photos of each other and enjoying the beautiful scenery.

Now he wanted to run 100 miles again. He had broken 24 hours on this course last time, and he hoped to do it again. I had paced him to the finish before, and of course I would help him this time, too.

Race day arrived. I was one of four people who would take turns pacing him. I waited for him about half-way, where pacing could begin. I hoped he would arrive about the same time as seven years ago, at dusk. That time came and went. Two and a half hours later, he reached the aid station and sat down.

I had his drop bag ready and asked what I could do to help. He was slow to respond. He said he had been held back by medical personnel at a previous aid station, but then allowed to continue. He had thought about dropping, but decided he just wouldn't do it.

I nudged him to think about what he wanted to do now, at this aid station. He said he wanted to change socks, and I would find them somewhere in his drop bag. As I opened that bag and rummaged through its five Ziploc bags, looking for the right one, he pondered what to eat and drink and wear. Time slipped away.

We finally left together, turned on our night lights, and trotted down a gentle grade. Gradually he moved faster, and we passed a couple of people. We stayed ahead of them on a long climb, and on the next smooth descent he stretched out and ran well, catching others. His old racing instincts kicked in as he sped up to make each pass decisive. He said he was running the best he had in the entire race.

Running downhill has always been his strength, and he talked about being puzzled earlier in the race when people passed him on downhill sections. But his shoulder had been injured from a fall during a training run, so he was concerned about tripping and falling again.

Fifteen miles later, we reached an aid station, where I said good-bye for now and handed him off to his next pacer. They headed out into the night on the most difficult section of the course, a trail filled with large rocks, roots, downed tress, constant turns, and sharp, short ups and downs. He remained positive and determined, but had trouble negotiating the tough terrain and was amazed when other runners passed him.

Deep in the night, he watched a tree morph into a Native American on horseback. Other fantastic figures floated across his eyes. A series of pacers ran with him through the night and next morning.

Late in the course, he reached a long, steep downhill section littered with rocks. When I had paced him there seven years ago, we had flown down together, and I'd run as hard as I could to keep up with him. This time, though, he moved carefully, trying not to fall. When he reached the bottom and the final aid station, listing to his left, our group of pacers joined him for the final few miles.

As we headed toward the finish line, he asked what time it was. When I told him, at first he didn't believe me. He had been working as hard as ever, doing his best, but for some reason the clock was running faster than it used to.

We still had enough time, though. He reached down and found a final pocket of energy to jog short sections with us, catching a couple of runners/walkers. Within sight of the finish line, a runner ahead of him looked back, saw us closing, and put on his own final kick to hold us off. My friend crossed the finish line with a smile of victory, slumped into a chair, and received his belt buckle.

While others attended to his needs, I walked away to a quiet place. I needed a few minutes alone to think about what I had just witnessed. When I had run with him in the past, his races were triumphs of his wonderful running talent and ability to run smartly. This run, however, was a triumph of his spirit.

It was his slowest 100-mile run, and in some ways his finest. I silently mourned the runner he once was, and celebrated the person he still is.

18 SLEEPLESS IN SPOKANE

George walked down the hall, looking for the air conditioning unit he was going to repair, saw me, and asked, "Why was the Energizer Bunny arrested?" I smiled, shrugged, and waited for his answer: "He was charged with battery."

Whenever we met, at school or church, George had a new joke. But that day he had more. "I hear you mountain bike," he said, "and you have friends who like to bike. What do you think about getting a team together to do a 24-hour mountain bike relay?" He told me about the event in Spokane in a couple of months. Most bikers would ride solo for the entire 24 hours, but six-person teams could also compete.

Why not? None of my friends or I had ever done an event like that, so I immediately said, "Let's do it." George found a friend, Ray, to ride, and I enlisted three friends I'd biked with— Tim Englund, Ethan Bergman, and Steve Varga.

Riding under our team name, Hot Dogs and Weenies (though none of us belonged in the first category), we drove to Spokane and found Riverside Park, a large, wooded area where the race would begin the next morning. We claimed a grassy spot near the start/finish line and hoisted our tents.

The instant I stepped inside my tent, I knew something was wrong. My sense of smell isn't what it once was, but even I could tell the tent reeked of something awful. *Maybe it just needs to air out, or maybe I'll get used to it.*

My teammates, though, also started gagging. While they pitched their tents upwind of mine, I figured it out. My tent had been stored all winter behind our house in an open shed where feral cats sometimes slept; at least one of them must have marked its territory, spraying my tent over and over again. *Not the best start to our race.*

In the early evening, we rode together to preview the course, a 12-mile loop. Someone scrounged up enough headlamps so we each had one, though several of us had never ridden in the dark using one. During the ride, we discovered a couple of hills where some of us decided we could climb faster if we just dismounted and ran our bikes up the steepest sections.

Soon we came to the dreaded piece, a steep, rooty, rocky descent called Devil's Down. I crashed partway down and decided discretion was the better part of valor. In fact, we all vowed that during the race we would dismount and walk our bicycles down that short section.

We returned to our tents for the night. All of us breathed comfortably except me. We each had a tent and Ray, George's friend, had the largest. Then I saw why. Ray shared his tent with Gisella, a friendly woman who had brought food from her home nearby and shared her German potato salad with all of us.

Race day was sunny. Dozens of bikers, most in garish shirts, congregated for the opening ceremonies. Then we were off. Ray, the closest we had to a Hot Dog, rode the first lap in just under an hour and finished near the back of the pack. Tim went next, and then Ethan. Our sequence was in order of ability. We didn't know how many laps our team would complete in 24 hours, but we wanted our strongest riders to go first so they would get their turns on the final rotation.

After finishing his first lap, Ray disappeared into the tent with Gisella and didn't emerge for a couple of hours. George started grousing for some reason. Meanwhile, we took our turns, each getting through the loop the best we could. When we weren't riding, we roamed the grounds, seeing the sights and trying to score as many free Clif Bars as our consciences and the booth attendants would allow.

Our first two rotations (twelve laps) went well. We were near the bottom of the standings, trailing all of the solo riders, even those using single-speed bicycles, but had our eyes on the same team everyone else was eyeing: The Trailer Trash Girls. The Girls were sporting fast outfits and slow bikes. It looked like the race for last place would come down to them and us.

After Ray returned from his third loop, in early evening, he declared he had successfully ridden the entire Devil's Down. When it was my turn, near midnight, I decided that if Ray could do it, so could I. Halfway down the Down, I went down. My bike, with its flat tire and mangled rear wheel, was now unridable. I scrambled to my feet and ran the last five miles, pushing my bicycle and setting a new record for slowness. When I finished, my teammates told me that the midnight chicken dinner provided for riders had just ended, but there was plenty of German potato salad left.

Soon Ray returned with Gisella from a trip to her house in Spokane, perhaps for rest and recreation, and took off on his next lap. George set up his bike stand, turned on a spotlight, and took out his tools to repair my bicycle. Still in a grumpy mood, he fixed the flat tire but couldn't straighten my wheel. He told me I was out of the race.

Ray's next loop took longer than usual. Feeling more confident about the Devil's Down, he rode it again, but fell near the bottom and found himself sitting in the dirt beside another fallen rider. Both had flat tires. The other rider was smoking a funny cigarette while he worked, and offered Ray some puffs. Soon Ray was very mellow, and his repair job showed it. When he resumed riding, Ray's tire went flat every mile or so, forcing him each time to dismount and pump it back up.

Ray finished his loop and drove off again with Gisella to her house while our team (now minus me) kept riding. As dawn broke, we were neck-and-neck (so to speak) with The Trailer Trash Girls. Final heroic rides by Tim and Ethan saved us from last place.

We broke camp. Ray left with Gisella. With joy, I pitched my still-reeking tent into the trash bin as the five of us drove away together. Then we learned why George, normally a good-natured fellow, had been so grumpy during the race: George and his wife were good friends with Ray and his wife, but Gisella was not Ray's wife.

At Ethan's suggestion, we stopped at Dick's Drive Inn, a Spokane landmark, to grab cheap eats before the long drive home. As we waited for our food George stared at sea gulls flying overhead and asked what we were doing in Seattle; we were supposed to be in Spokane for a bike ride. The rest of us looked at each other, confused.

Then we realized George was slipping into a diabetic coma, probably from taking his insulin without ingesting enough carbohydrates. We stopped by the emergency room at a nearby hospital, but George refused to go in. Finally, Ethan got him to drink some juice, hoping that his problem was a low blood sugar level. That did the trick, quickly transforming George back to normal.

Our hunger pangs returned during the three-hour drive back to Ellensburg. Ethan rescued us by announcing that his wife's relatives were holding a family reunion in Ephrata, where there should be lots of free food. We changed our route slightly to go there, crashed the party, and like a horde of locusts devoured everything left on the table, while adding our aromas to those of the casseroles, beans and Jell-Os.

The next few years, Ethan was told that there wasn't a family reunion.

19 RAGBRAI

Laurae and I were visiting my sister, Lois, and her husband, Carlton, in Iowa. Lois started talking about when I had gotten lost in a whiteout and spent eighteen hours shivering in a snow hole, curled up in a fetal position. She was one of the people I had driven to the airport that fateful morning, before I started running back to Ellensburg. She had caught her flight, arrived home, and then heard from Laurae that I had been caught in a snowstorm during my run and was missing. She told me the rest of her story.

"I worried about you all night," she began. "The next morning, I had to go to work at a nursing home. That's where I was when I heard that Search and Rescue had found you and you were going to be okay. I was so happy I just couldn't help but talk to the residents, telling them how my brother had been lost, but now was found. I really poured my heart out to them. When I finished, the room was silent. Then one of the residents, an elderly lady with a puzzled look on her face, raised her hand and asked, 'How big was that fish?'"

After we finished laughing, Lois said: "Now that you're doing bike rides, too, why don't you come out here next summer and ride your bicycle across the state? Laurae and I will drive along and meet you each night at a campsite. I've done the ride, and I know it will be fun." I thought, *What's not to like?*

In 1973, two writers for the *Des Moines Register*, the state's largest newspaper, decided to bicycle across Iowa with some invited friends and write about their trip. RAGBRAI (the *Register*'s Annual Great Bicycle Ride across Iowa) was born. The event had grown to about 10,000 registered cyclists doing the complete ride each year, plus two to three thousand unregistered ones (bandits), plus others registered to pedal a day or two of the seven-day event.

The route changed each year as towns vied for the honor and commercial bonanza of hosting the event. The next year, when I signed up, the course followed roads just north of Interstate 80. As usual, we would begin near the western border (Missouri River) and pedal to the eastern border (Mississippi River) almost 500 miles away.

So the next summer Laurae and I drove to Iowa, picked up Lois, and kept driving until we reached the massive campsite where the ride would start. The mob of people startled me. *How can I possibly avoid an accident with so many other riders?*

In the morning I crawled out of my tent at 5:30 a.m., downed a Frappuccino for breakfast, and started riding at 6. Laurae and

Lois woke up later, ate breakfast, and meandered along on parallel roads (cars weren't allowed on the bike route), taking their sweet time, enjoying the day, and eventually meeting me at the next campsite. This would be our pattern every day.

The event began at Missouri Valley with a 59-mile ride on a roller-coaster road (yes, Iowa has hills) with almost 4000 feet of climb. *No need to follow maps or signs; just follow the armada of bikers.* I cruised along on my mountain bike and kept to the right side of the pavement, letting others, mostly on road bikes, pass on the left. Twice we rode past clusters of bleeding bikers sprawled on the highway, their downed bikes scattered or tangled, and heard ambulance sirens.

Bicyclists streamed past. One shirt proclaimed "Blazing Saddle;" another said "Aorta Be Biking." A fit, grey-haired woman shot by with her shirt declaring: "Chain Smoker." Two women of similar age rode a tandem with a sign bearing a 2007 date and the words: "Almost Married." Every few miles brought a chance to eat and drink: smoothies, cookies, pork chops, pie ala mode, and my favorite of the day—fresh corn on the cob.

Afternoon brought us into Harlan, the end of the day's ride. Many fine churches on nicely landscaped grounds suggested this was one God-fearing (or loving) town. Of course; it's Iowa. A note on the message board told me where to meet Laurae and Lois, and I finally spotted them in the sea of tents dotting a grassy area.

At 2:30 a.m., a vehicle with a loudspeaker woke us up, blaring that a storm was coming; we had to vacate our tents and find shelter. Camped along Cyclone Avenue, we readily complied. *How many people can you crowd into a one-sink men's rest room by the grandstand of the fairgrounds? Not nearly enough.*

The climb (5300 feet) and distance (83 miles), made the next day's ride the second toughest in the 36-year history of RAGBRAI. The first six hours continued the hilly terrain of the first day as we enjoyed the sights and smells of Iowa. Lush corn and soy bean crops filled the horizon. As for smells, local aficionados said they could tell the difference between hog and cow manure. Depending on which "expert" you asked, the cow product smelled (a) cleaner, (b) yuckier, or (c) less intense (because of rules that allow hogs to be kept closer together).

Signs of "Wellkomen" greeted us as we entered Kimballton and Elk Horn, home of the largest rural Danish population in the country. There our breakfast options included aebleskivers, golf-ball-shaped pancakes. Back on the road, a woman wearing an enormous bra stuffed with something cycled by, showing some sign about women's health (probably breast cancer) and in large letters: "Save the Tatas." One guy rode a unicycle, while another zoomed by on a recumbent bike entirely encased as a Chiquita banana.

After 57 miles we reached Coon Rapids, refueled for the umpteenth time, and watched Elvis perform on stage in the town square. That town, like the others, resembled a county fair, with endless food booths jammed with happy customers. Stands also offered bicycle repair, temporary bicycle tattoos, and thongs to wear under biking shorts to prevent those dreaded underwear lines. Portable toilets were everywhere.

Leaving town, we saw damage from last night's storm. Straight-line winds that reached 80 mph had uprooted trees, blown down a silo, and flattened cornfields that no longer provided adequate cover for emergency pit stops. I thought of a sign I'd seen earlier in the day: "What Happens in an Iowa Corn Field Stays in an Iowa Corn Field."

Near the end of the day's long ride, a passing biker proclaimed his need for a butt transplant. *The agony of de seat.* Conversations dwindled as riders conserved their remaining energy. Just before Jefferson, our finishing town, we passed through Scranton, where we were delayed by a long train. A local explained that 78 trains roll through Scranton each day.

I found Laurae and Lois, ate a church dinner, and crumpled into the tent.

On day three, we pedaled into Ogden and watched Elvis, who had added a few inches and pounds since yesterday, again performing on stage. *He must like Iowa.* Breakfast options included a walking taco—ground beef or chili, shredded cheese, and optional onions added to the chips in a small Fritos bag. Aficionados recommended that before you ate it (with a plastic fork), the mixture should be shaken, not stirred.

I sat down to eat next to several clients of Pork Belly travel, some of the 700 riders in their group who were met at the airport in Omaha, transported to the start of the ride, provided sleeping accommodations during the ride and breakfast each day, and driven back to the airport when the ride ended. In addition, their package included bicycle mechanics and massage services. I also learned about Team Cuisine—a smaller group that had split off from Team Gourmet—whose members stayed in homes in the local towns each night and dined on food prepared by their own chef.

Fifty-seven fairly flat miles made for a relatively easy day except for 15-mph headwinds. As we cycled through small towns, the welcomes included: the mayor handing out popsicles; local cheerleaders cheering; people in lawn chairs saying "welcome;" and kids handing out goodies or looking for high fives. The only alarming note was seeing greeters wearing shirts advertising a local funeral home. I asked them if RAGBRAI was good for business.

Ten miles from the day's finish line, I couldn't resist stopping for a root beer float and conversation. Riders had come from all fifty states and many countries. Their median age was 40-something, and about 30% were women. I met Iowans from all over, and learned that each one lived in the nicest town in their state.

Camp was waiting at 1 p.m. in Ames, the largest overnight town and home to Iowa State University. Riders were spread out here and we lost our sense of community. Dinner at a local church was followed by a Styx concert to benefit Iowans recovering from recent floods. The concert raised $100,000 and included Lance Armstrong, making his annual appearance at RAGBRAI.

Early the next day, we pedaled out of Ames into a sun just peeking over the horizon on a cool, cloudless morning. The road was remarkably clean, having just been swept and the cracks filled. Several years earlier, a RAGBRAI rider had hit a road crack, fallen and died. The lawsuit had been recently settled for $375,000, so extra care was taken to make the roads immaculate.

Almost. A few miles out of Ames, about fifteen riders were off the road repairing flat tires, courtesy of some lowlife who had scattered tacks on the road earlier in the morning. Signs told us to have breakfast in six miles with the Bare Naked Ladies. The ladies did indeed turn out to be naked—from the neck up. *The truth-in-advertising people need to speak to them.*

In Colo, a spot in the road, $4 bought me two huge pancakes, two sausages and coffee. And a chance to be saved. As I ate, a local evangelist gave me Bible literature and told me where I could pray, while a 13-year-old girl on stage played the fiddle and testified about the Lord. I left before the altar call.

On our bicycles we wore license plates listing our names and home states. Back on the road, a sweet, innocent voice read my plate and said, "Hello, David," as she passed by. She was maybe ten years old, in seat three on a long bike, with Dad in front, followed by young brother, and Mom in seat four. When other bikers saw I was from Washington, their most common comment was: "That's a beautiful state."

After 73 miles on a pleasant but humid day with another headwind, we pedaled five miles across Meskwaki land, the only Native American settlement in the state. A passing biker explained that much of the land we "gave" the Meskwakis was a swamp, and they deserved better. Their casino was supposed to make things fair.

The twin towns of Tama and Toledo provided excellent camping. Laurae and Lois had grabbed a prime spot and were smiling when I arrived. They'd enjoyed a fine day of leisurely driving, shopping along the way, and sampling Indian tacos (Indian fried bread with taco fixings).

The next morning, I awakened in a tent wet from the night's rain. Our congregation of bikers pedaled under a cloudy sky that masked sunrise. The usual signs appeared. In five miles came Little Farm's self-serve, self-pay, fresh, water-filtered, organic, gourmet, fair-trade coffee. Further down the road were the Farm Boys, featuring their breakfast burritos, highly recommended by my friend, Bob Kuhlken, who had ridden RAGBRAI the previous year. (Bob also recommended Biker Butt'r, but not to eat.)

If you were looking for ethnic diversity, you came to the wrong place. Among the few African-American riders, several sported U.S. Air Force Cycling Team jerseys. The most popular bike brands seemed to be Trek, Cannondale and Specialized, while Burley ruled the tandem division. Very few rode mountain bikes.

A burly biker had a decal on his shirt that said "Illinois Police" and the team name: "Guns N' Hoses." At the Czech community of Vining, two French toast, a large sausage patty and coffee set me back $2. Light rain and another headwind forced a variety of clothing decisions on the cool, 75-mile day.

After pie ala mode at the next town (*it's a tough job, but someone has to do it*), we reached the Amana colonies: West Amana, South Amana and Homestead. The first two had no commercial activity, in marked contrast to every other town we had passed through. But at Homestead, one of the original settlements, the picture of a simple, wholesome lifestyle unencumbered by the modern world was shattered. A rock-and-roll band blasted away in a well-attended beer garden, while two dozen booths were hawking the usual stuff. The real residents of Homestead seemed to have fled town for the day.

I passed by the beer gardens, which were highly recommended by my friend, Mel van Houten, who had done the ride several years earlier with his wife, Keiko. *I can't keep pace with Mel at either biking or drinking.*

All day long, every day, Iowa patrol officers at road junctions kept traffic moving and safe. When we said, "Thank you," they responded with, "You're welcome" (early in the day) or "Yep" (late in the day) with the occasional "You betcha." Also busy were the SAG wagons, which transported to the finish line people (and their bicycles) who couldn't finish the day's ride.

In North Tipton, we camped and enjoyed another church dinner, enabling us by then to compare the culinary offerings of the Church of Christ, Lutherans, Methodists, Presbyterians, Roman Catholics and Seventh Day Adventists. My apologies to those we missed.

Day six brought another 64 miles. After twenty, did I want fresh-baked kolaches—bread rolls filled with fruit and/or cheese—or cinnamon rolls with my coffee? While I refueled, I spotted an older couple watching the spectacle astride their side-by-side tandem bicycle. Our city on wheels then rolled across the swollen Cedar River, which had recently overrun that part of Iowa. Small, temporary lakes still flanked its low banks.

The Burma-Shave-style signs were relentless. They proclaimed the wonders and environmental virtues of the state's pork and asphalt industries. They told us what vendor was coming up next, and many ended in exclamation points to tell us—in case we hadn't noticed—how cleverly they were worded!!!!

At booths along the road, we could donate to many worthy causes: Iowa Flood Relief, Amy's College Fund, Autism/Fragile X Syndrome. *The best money-raiser today would be donations to cure Fragile Butt Syndrome.*

I'd been avoiding it all week, but I finally took the plunge and visited Mr. Pork Chop. Beginning in 1983, Paul Bernhard had been at every RAGBRAI at a stand with his pink bus announcing with a guttural voice: "POOORK CHOOOOPP." When he reached 80 years old, he turned the business over to his son. You knew you were getting close to their stand—like many others, located at the top of a hill where you're going slow and needing a break—because the billowing smoke from their corn-cob-fueled fire made you think a house was on fire. I bought a tasty, one-inch thick slab of meat and a napkin, sat down on the grass, and sent it down to my protesting stomach. I staggered to my feet and rode on.

Near the end of the day's ride, I pedaled alongside Jim, a paraplegic who was able to hand-crank his machine. A graduate in Forestry from Washington State University, he worked for the

Bureau of Indian Affairs in New Mexico. This was his fifth RAGBRAI, and he had completed every day of each one. He knew the other paraplegics here by name. Good conversation made the final miles disappear in our wake.

That night, like every night, was party time. We apparently camped too close to the band stand, because at something o'clock I awakened to the sounds of one camper distressed over her lost wallet while others in a nearby tent were arguing about polygamy. Providing background music to all this excitement was a band that must have placed 199th in the Iowan Idol competition (though first in the loud and enthusiastic category) belting out their 16th consecutive chorus of: "Everybody's gone surfin', surfin' I-O-Way." *The Beach Boys must be very proud.*

Our final day arrived. A few vendors had already left. On this relatively short, 51-mile ride, near the top of a hill, we heard, "Biker down." A man lay motionless on the road while someone administered CPR. I heard "Heart attack," and "He's not breathing," and then an ambulance siren. *Good luck, my friend.*

We rode through New Liberty, awash with American flags, and ate breakfast. Later we passed a stand offering Grandma's Cookies for $1 and no charge for Grandma's Stories and Grandma's Secrets of Life. A smiling lady, her grey hair swept into a bun, awaited her customers.

The finish line approached. Laurae and Lois were waiting for me at Le Claire, where I plunged down to the eastern border of Iowa and honored the custom of dipping my bicycle tires in the Mississippi River. The party was over.

As we packed up to drive home, we noticed in the parking lot a motor home carrying a large sign. What it said about RAGBRAI neatly summarized how I felt, not only about the event, but also about more than three decades of getting to experience wonderful adventures on foot and bicycle. The sign said:

Bike—$1000

Registration—$150

Showers—$5

RAGBRAI—Priceless

20 ZULULAND ODYSSEY

After races, we would pile into somebody's car to drive home.
Conversation would be easy and predictable. Who did you meet
on the trail today? How did your run go? What went well and
what didn't? What did you learn, and what will you do differently
next time?

Eventually, our conversation would fade as we succumbed to
fatigue. But we still had many miles to go, and we needed to keep
the driver awake. So we'd ask other questions of each other:
What is your greatest fear, your favorite book, your most precious
possession, your best run? Of all the people in the world, not
counting those you know personally or are related to, who do you
admire the most?

My answer to the last question was easy: Nelson Mandela,
affectionately known as Madiba, his Xosa clan name. He was
imprisoned for 27 years, 18 of them at notorious Robben Island,
before leading his country to overthrow apartheid. But it's what
he did after becoming President of South Africa in 1994-1999 that
truly set him apart. Once in power, he sought not revenge but

reconciliation with the white population that had so abused him and all other blacks in the country. One example, portrayed in the movie *Invictus*, is when his country hosted the World Cup of rugby in 1995. Mandela, newly elected as President, urged his black countrymen and women to support the previously hated (and previously all-white) national rugby team, which became world champions that year. For me, Mandela exemplified leadership, dignity, forgiveness and humility.

Mandela resonates with me because I lived some of my first years in South Africa, where my father was a missionary to Zulu people. Our family returned to the U.S. in 1949, and my father's first task, as pastor of a congregation in Omaha, Nebraska, was to integrate that church, which he did.

Mom got into the act, too. For my ninth birthday, she took the friends at my party, including several black children, to a roller skating rink. When the proprietor said the white kids could skate but not the black ones, she replied, "Either we all skate or none of us skate." Money trumped bigotry that day. We all skated.

The struggle of blacks for equality, in South Africa and in our country, was gaining momentum, but had a long way to go. When my uncle, a native white South African minister, visited us and accompanied my father to speak at the local Rotary Club, my father suffered in silence as my uncle explained what virtually all white South Africans believed at the time: "The racial policy of apartheid is necessary because blacks don't have the experience, education and knowledge to govern South Africa."

Things changed, of course, when apartheid was finally overthrown and Mandela became President. So it was a happy surprise when my mother, Esther, told her two sons and two daughters that she was paying for us to travel back to our roots of 55 years ago. We would see where we lived, worship at the Zulu church my father helped establish, meet missionary relatives (who now largely work with AIDS patients), and visit game reserves and other sites of interest.

Then in my 60s, I thought about Comrades, the oldest and largest ultramarathon in the world, attracting 15,000 or so runners each year. That event—about 54 miles between the cities of Pietermaritzburg and Durban (the direction alternates each year)—was established in 1921 as a living memorial to soldiers who served in World War I. The race has been held every year since then except 1941-45, during World War II. Blacks could only run unofficially before 1975, and some did. After that, the name also reflected the fact that, even in the terrible shadow of apartheid (which ended in 1994), Comrades was one place where people of all races could meet and compete.

Since my brother had Parkinson's disease, we decided to travel as soon as possible. I asked if we could time our trip so I could run Comrades, and my siblings agreed. As luck would have it, I drew the slightly faster, "downhill" route, ending in Durban.

The four of us flew from our respective homes (Carol in New Hampshire, Lois in Iowa, John in Minnesota and me in Washington) to meet in Atlanta, where we caught an 18-hour flight to Johannesburg, South Africa, and then another flight to Durban. There we were met by 70-year-old Solveig Otte, a life-long resident of South Africa and family friend who would stay with us for several days.

She took us to see Mpophomeni, a town created during apartheid to house only blacks, and that still had only black residents. That town of 40,000 people had no recognizable stores, not even a grocery store; several houses, though, were known to be places where people could buy a few things to eat. We visited two crèches (preschools) and saw well-dressed Zulu children with great smiles and sparkling eyes, eager to learn.

Solveig told us that the unemployment rate there was 82%. Sixty percent of the residents, including 25% of their beautiful children, had the AIDS virus. All around town were graveyards with freshly turned dirt. Solveig explained that funeral homes were one of the most thriving businesses in South Africa.

We visited a prosperous farm and its white owners of Boer (Dutch) descent. The farm had been in their family for several generations. The owner showed us an elementary school he had built on his property that educated about 100 black children.

When I asked if he feared the government would confiscate his land and give it to black owners, he replied: "If that happens, I know I will be compensated fairly, and that the new owners will probably hire me to manage the land because I know how to do that. We are not like some other countries in Africa."

We spent a night with Solveig at her home in Pietermaritzburg, where Comrades would begin the next day. Early in the cool, clear morning, she drove me to the starting area. I found my "corral," the place I was to start based on my marathon qualifying time. In predawn darkness, the mayor of Pietermaritzburg fired a gun from atop the portico of the historic City Hall, and we were off.

Our mass of humanity inched forward. After 20 minutes, I could run somewhat freely, and for 90 chilly minutes I saw my breath. The city streets, even at 5:30 a.m., were jammed with people tooting horns, banging drums, and cheering. Children lined the road, their hands out, seeking contact with runners.

Comrades originally had an 11-hour time limit, but had recently increased it to 12. In my younger days, I would have tried for the special medals given to those who finish under nine, and even seven, hours, but now my goal was to beat the original time limit and, most of all, savor the experience.

The number of runners was striking. Unlike any other ultramarathon I had ever run, I could always see hundreds of runners ahead as we ran the paved, roller-coaster road. At Inchanga, children from the Ethembeni home leaned on crutches or sat in wheelchairs, cheering us as we streamed past.

At Drummond, about half-way and with a marathon left to run, I was hurting. The relentless hills (surprisingly many going up on this "downhill" course) and constant pounding on pavement hammered my legs, and my stomach was rebelling against all the liquid fuel I was forcing down my throat. I took an extended walk break, downed two ibuprofen tablets, and drank only water. In half an hour I was running again.

Aid stations appeared every mile, complete with at least thirty volunteers. At many, especially those late in the race, volunteers also stood ready to massage aching bodies. The liquids—water, Coke and a local energy drink—were handed to us as liquid sausages encased in thin plastic. I learned to gnaw a corner of the plastic, squeeze liquid into my mouth, and then discard the plastic. A million plastic casings dotted the road to Durban.

More than a million spectators watched us. In towns, the crowds swelled. On this national holiday (Youth Day), people crowded along the route everywhere, having picnics and cheering the runners. Radio stations broadcasting from the event provided ear-splitting renditions of such African classics as "Pretty Woman" and "We Will Rock You."

A nearby woman runner, wearing a shirt that said "Australia," prompted many cheers of "Go Australia." I kept a low profile, since Solveig had told me that most South Africans—of all colors—thought U.S. actions in Iraq were unjustified. But when runners asked me where I was·from, and I told them, they all treated me with warm hospitality.

On bone-tired legs, I reached Durban and ran into Kingsmead cricket stadium, filled to capacity with 30,000 people. I crossed the finish line in 10:26, in the middle of the pack. Fifteen minutes later, I could hardly believe what I heard over the PA system: a man had just finished his 40th Comrades. *Amazing.* I found my brother and sisters and we sat in the infield, having a bite to eat and watching the finish of the spectacle.

Comrades is the most-watched television event in South Africa. Coverage had been continuous for nine hours, and the images were projected on a massive screen in the stadium. As usual, the final person to finish, and the first person not to finish, would be interviewed.

Ten minutes before the 12-hour time limit, the 12-hour "bus" (runners carrying a 12-hour sign that other runners could use for pacing) entered the stadium, followed by 2000 runners. With less than a lap to the finish line, all 2000 finished in time.

But runners continued to trickle in. The crowd cheered and screamed, urging them to reach the finish line in time. A uniformed official, his back to the runners, stepped out and faced the clock as it counted down. At exactly 12 hours, a horn would be blown, after which he would no longer allow runners to cross the finish line.

As the final minute ticked down, several runners were on the track, desperately trying to finish. One of them, an older woman, was just thirty yards from the finish line when she heard the dreaded horn. No longer having a reason to will her body forward, she crumpled to the track and lay motionless.

We climbed out of the steeply-tiered stadium, having to negotiate several flights of stairs. All were partially blocked by runners who had collapsed and were awaiting medical help. A dozen bodies were being carried on stretchers as we exited the stadium.

Walking back to our hotel, we got lost. Three Indian policemen spotted us and told us it wasn't safe to be in this part of town in late afternoon. We couldn't all fit into the police car, so two officers drove my sisters to our hotel while the other stayed with my brother and me. When the policemen returned and picked us up, they gave us, as they had given my sisters, a wild ride, ignoring speed limits and red lights, clearly enjoying showing us that they were the law.

Comrades was unforgettable, but the best was yet to come. On a sunny Sunday morning, we siblings visited Ntunjambili, where we had grown up nearly six decades ago. We walked through our long-ago home, seeing where we spent many happy hours with Funani, our Zulu nanny, and the room where our mother had home-schooled us.

We sat outside on the verandah, savoring memories: where we painted captured monkeys yellow before releasing them to deter other monkeys from poaching our fruit; the distant Tugela river, where my father, on hikes to outlying Zulu villages, knelt to pray for protection against crocodiles before wading across; the place near the porch where our Doberman pincer stepped between a black mamba and my three-year-old sister, Carol, saving her life; and my terror in the bouncing bed of a pick-up truck trying to outrun a charging rhinoceros my father and uncle had been hunting.

Before the church service began, we walked into the cemetery and noticed the graves of a white woman and her daughter. When we asked why the husband wasn't buried with them, our guide, an elderly Zulu man, explained that Peter Reid had died after his wife and daughter had been buried, and after a new apartheid law had been passed banning whites from black churches and their cemeteries. The day of Peter Reid's funeral, many of his Zulu friends had come to this church, only to learn that they had to walk another six miles to the nearest white church. Once there, they had to stand outside the church during the funeral service, and then outside the cemetery as Peter's remains were laid to rest alongside other whites, instead of those of his wife and daughter. The Zulu man explained, with quiet dignity and without a trace of bitterness in his voice, "It's just the way things were."

My brother, two sisters, and I entered the church where our father had preached, nearly the only whites among 200 people, for a two-hour service without microphones or musical accompaniment. The church was clean and dignified. Women wore dresses, or white blouses and black skirts, and men wore dark suit coats, white shirts and neckties. They punctuated the long sermon with "yes" or "m-hm" to voice their approval.

Near the end of the service, the native pastor, a woman of generous circumference, introduced us to the congregation and asked us to sing for them, as we had anticipated. We sang, unaccompanied and in four-part harmony, a familiar hymn. When we finished, the congregation sang back to us, in Zulu and with rich, joyful, resonant harmony, the same hymn: "It Is Well With My Soul."

It is, indeed.

21 SLOWER MILES

One day Laurae asked, "What's left on your bucket list?"

I thought about it and replied, "Nothing."

After running Comrades in South Africa, the only other run I had really wanted to do someday was the Boston Marathon. So I qualified for that race and traveled with running friends to Boston. The experience and crowds there were as great as I had hoped. Most memorable was about midway in the race, when we passed Wellesley College. The young women cheered us on and held up signs saying "Kiss Me." So I did. Then I noticed some of them putting away their signs.

After completing the Great Divide Ride, I didn't have any biking routes on my bucket list, either, though there were plenty I'd like to do. In fact, I'm currently riding, in sections each summer with friends, the Sierra Cascade Route, which runs parallel to the Pacific Crest Trail from the Canadian to Mexican border.

The closest thing to something left on my bucket list was to hike the Appalachian Trail. But instead of wanting to *hike* the

Appalachian Trail, I realized I really would like to *have hiked* it. Frankly, I'd rather run and bike than carry a pack on my back.

It's just as well there's nothing left on my list. Because as I get older, I'm learning what every other runner and biker my age knows: even if you work hard to stay in shape, you eventually lose speed and strength. The number of people completing long-distance runs, for example, plummets after age 60 and nearly vanishes after age 70. And if you find names with those ages at all, they will be near the bottom of the list of finishers. Bicycling, however, is a bit more forgiving.

Father Time extracts a toll. In fact, Father Time is undefeated. A lean, older friend of mine who runs regularly had a physical assessment and was shocked at his high percentage of body fat. He learned, to his dismay, that even if you stay the same weight as you get older (and most of us don't), your percent of body fat increases while your percent of muscle declines. No wonder you lose strength and speed.

Aging is inevitable. How you handle it is up to you.

As far as I know, I'm the first male in my family tree whose age begins with a 7. My father died at 65, four days after he retired. Both of my grandfathers died younger than that. Have I reached this age, at least in part, because of all my running and biking adventures, and the physical training that makes them possible?

The answer probably is "yes," but I'm not sure, for at least two reasons. First, what I know about my ancestry is limited because I'm just not that interested in genealogy. One year my brother did many hours of research, constructed a beautiful, elaborate family tree going back many generations, and sent it to me for Christmas. I looked at it, thanked him, put it in a nice frame, and hung it in a hallway near the bathroom.

My only real interest in genealogy is to find genetic information that could affect my health. What my recent family history says is that I'm most likely to die, like my father and his father did, from a heart attack.

The second reason I'm not sure my active lifestyle gives me more years is that studies on this subject aren't entirely conclusive. It seems obvious that physical activity should be good for our hearts and lungs and keep our weight down; as a result, we should have a lower risk of dying early because of heart disease or diseases (such as type-2 diabetes) associated with obesity.

Some studies do show modest correlations between physical aerobic activity (such as running and bicycling) and longevity, but even those don't prove that physical activity *causes* increased lifespan. Correlations don't prove cause-and-effect. For example, people who enjoy excellent health, thanks to great genetics and reasonable diets, may naturally live longer and also be more physically active; this could be another reason for the correlation. It's a chicken-and-egg question.

Although it seems obvious that physical activity should help us live longer, let me, just for a minute, put on my biochemistry cap. It turns out there's a dark side to the aerobic coin.

When we breathe hard from physical work, we send more oxygen coursing through our bodies to burn fuel for our muscles to work. As a result, our hearts and lungs and other body parts get stronger. That's the good news. The not-so-good news, however, is that when our bodies use oxygen, a small but unavoidable percentage of that oxygen is converted into toxic byproducts (called free radicals) that harm our tissues and organs. Much of this damage is repaired, but not all of it. So over time it builds up.

An important theory of aging is that the accumulating free radical damage causes aging and sets an upper limit (110-120 years) on how long anyone can live, even under the best of conditions. It's ironic: the same oxygen that keeps us alive limits how long we can live. More aerobic exercise means more oxygen. In other words, every breath I take brings in oxygen that (to borrow words sung by Roberta Flack) is "killing me softly," though ever so slowly.

So slowly, though, that I'm not worried about it. We are still likely to live longer if we have physically active lives because we will lower our risk of dying early from diseases. If that costs us a few years on our maximum life span, reducing that to, say, 100-105 years, most of us will come out ahead in the bargain.

We'll come out farther ahead for another reason. While I'm not sure my adventures give me a much longer life, I am sure they give me a much better quality of life. Losing weight is why I started running, but that has become a secondary (though welcome) reason to keep running and biking. Now I do those things mostly for sheer pleasure.

I started running, and then bicycling, to help take care of my body, but little did I know it would also help take care of my mind. When I was stewing over some problem at work, sometimes for weeks, running relieved my stress and gave me new perspective. Often I would return from a run realizing that my problem was not as earth-shaking as I had believed. I simply needed to make the best decision I could and then move on.

Once you get in good shape, your body can operate on automatic pilot. I remember day-dreaming during one run and being startled to discover where I was on the course. For many miles my body had freed my mind to go elsewhere.

Running alone gives you solitude, a break from the rest of the world, and a time to think. When I started running long distances, almost all of my training runs were alone because no one else in town ran that far. I was fine with that. After a few years some friends started joining me on my runs. I was fine with that, too.

Now my runs are slower. My friends, because they are friends, sometimes slow their pace to keep me company. But I don't really want to keep them from running as well as they can, and I don't want the pressure of trying to keep up with them by running faster than I now can.

On a recent Saturday run in the woods, I said good-bye to my friends after a few minutes and watched them run on ahead. During the next three hours I thought about how my ultrarunning years have come full circle: from running alone, to running with others, to running alone again.

Was it (in the words of Alan Sillitoe) "the loneliness of the long distance runner?" Not really. I was alone, but I wasn't lonely. My company was solitude, an overcast sky, flora and fauna all around, and a creek running beside me. *Not bad at all.*

With or without company, I've experienced the simple joy of running. My day job—working with students to develop their skills in reasoning and logic—was largely a life of the mind. But running awakened some deep, primordial instinct within my body. It unleashed the animal inside and somehow made me a more complete person.

You also learn life lessons when you try to do something as difficult as running and bicycling long distances. I learned, for example, that the longer the distance and the tougher the terrain, the more important it is to train hard and make good decisions during the run or ride. And the more challenging the course, the more satisfaction you get when you finish.

In long distance running, as in life, you mostly get what you earn. If you take short cuts in training, the only person you're cheating is yourself. And when the going gets tough, in training and in races, you learn to take one mile at a time or, if that's too much, keep going to the next tree (and then the next one). That attitude—handling just five minutes at a time when necessary— helped me get through some very dark days when I went through chemotherapy for cancer.

Good athletes are a product both of their genetics and training. You get your genetics, for better or worse, for free. Part of life is finding out what we're naturally good at. When we discover those things, we tend to enjoy doing them. Then we get even better at them.

My friend, Larry Almberg, was a collegiate steeplechase champion, set a U.S. Master's (over age 40) record in the mile (4:06), and his Portland Marathon Master's record is still standing after 25 years. His eyes lit up when he told me about the day he discovered he was a winner in the genetic lottery for runners. In fourth grade, his teacher told everyone in his class to line up and run across a field to a tree and back. When he finished, the light bulb went on in his head when he turned around and saw he was way ahead of the next runner.

After college, Larry stopped running. More than a decade later, he started running again, shortly after I started. We drove together to a 10-km race, and I beat him. We had a very quiet drive home. Then he started training in earnest. Although my racing times kept improving, I never came close to beating him again.

The very best athletes are genetically gifted and train very hard. If you want to win an Olympic gold medal, you first need to choose your parents very carefully. Then you have to train like crazy. But I discovered that, in long-distance running, even those of us who don't inherit four aces can perform well by training hard and playing our cards wisely during the event. We can still cross the finish line fully satisfied.

Now the pepper in my beard is turning into salt and my hair is thinning. As I get slower, I still run as long as I ever did; I just don't go as far. Satchel Paige, the famous Negro League baseball player who was the oldest pitcher (at age 42) to make his Major League debut, famously said: "Don't look back. Something might be gaining on you."

As I move nearer the back of the pack in races, I now have to say: "Don't look back; nobody's there."

I know several people older than me who still run long distances. When I asked one how much longer he can keep doing it, he replied: "I don't ask that question. Instead, every morning I get up, think about my workout, and say: 'I can do that today.'"

It must be harder for truly elite athletes, like Larry, to keep racing once they get old. They are used to the excitement of competing to be the overall winner, so it must be hard when they no longer can be in the front of the pack. I don't have the same burden. As I slip back in the pack, maybe it's easier for me to accept my declining performance and be at peace with the simple joy of running or bicycling in beautiful places and with friends.

My attitude began to change in 1994, the third time I ran the Western States 100-Mile Endurance Run. I'd had some disappointing races, including a couple I didn't finish, so I decided that year at Western States I was going to enjoy the run, no matter how long it took.

I started at a leisurely pace, embracing the beautiful scenery. As day turned into night, I noticed at aid stations that I was catching up to the pace needed to earn the 24-hour silver belt buckle. But I kept running at a comfortable pace, reveling in my surroundings. In the final two miles, reaching pavement and hiking up Robie Point, a spectator told me I could break 24 hours if I ran hard to the finish. I thought about it, and then kept walking. *I'm going to enjoy this run, no matter what.* When I got to the top of the hill, though, I threw my fanny pack on the ground to lighten the load and ran down to the finish line. As luck would have it, I was the final person that day to break 24 hours, with a minute and change to spare.

My running pace now is governed less by a stopwatch than by Father Time. At 24-hour events, 100 miles is out of reach, though I still try to run as long and far as I can. I'm sometimes the oldest runner at races, and I shake my head at the times I used to run, thinking about what someone once said: "The older I get, the faster I was."

Although I started out a runner, bicycling has become a wonderful addition to my quality of life, especially as I get older. Indeed, I expect my running days will end before my bicycling days do. Each summer, when my training changes from running to biking, the first time I get on my bicycle, I think: *Biking is sure easier than running*. And each autumn, when I return to running, my first impression is: *Running is sure harder than biking*.

Running and bicycling adventures, though, have much in common. With both I get the excitement of going someplace new, being outdoors, working my body, taking the weather and other challenges as they come, and sharing the experiences with like-minded people. Sometimes things go badly; sometimes they go well. But the pain, when it comes, is temporary. The satisfaction, memories and friendships last a lifetime.

The mountains and valleys, rivers and streams, trails and roads, creatures great and small, summer and winter, still call my name, inviting me outside to enjoy the pleasure of their company. Whether on foot or bicycle, I get to channel my inner hobo, which, for me, means freedom: freedom to go where I want, when I want, and to choose (in the fine words of Robert Frost) how many "miles to go before I sleep."

When I started running, each week day I would go over to the locker room at our gym and always see Don Ringe and George Macinko. Both were fine collegiate athletes who were teaching at our university, Don in geology and George in geography. George usually worked out with weights or the wrestling team, while Don did both weights and aerobic exercises. Don gave me the locker used by his son, a national-level discus thrower, who had graduated and was going on to his doctoral studies.

When I turned 40, I watched Don and George, then in their early 50s, working out, and said to myself, "I want to be like them when I'm 50." When I was 50, they were still there, and I said to myself, "I want to be like them when I'm 60." When I turned 60, I watched them and said to myself, "I want to be like them when I'm 70." About that time George, then in his early 70s, traveled to Europe to compete in his age group in weight lifting and came home a world champion.

Now I go over to the gym, nearly every week day, and usually see Don and George working out. Here I am, 71 years old, and I still want to be like them when I grow up.

ACKNOWLEDGMENTS

Thanks to my wife, Laurae, for the painting and to Edna and Eilert Bjorge and Kirsten Cox for their technical and artistic skills in transforming that picture into the cover for this book. Kirsten also provided valuable technical help for my website (davidlygre.com) and for publishing this book.

I'm grateful to all the people who have enriched my life while running and bicycling with me. In addition to those named in this book, they include William Holmes, Scott Sparks, Judie Boman, Bob Carbaugh, Phil Tolin, Bill Allison, Bill Boyum, Gary Schmid, Lisa Bliss, Max Welker, John Bandur, Wayne Quirk, Barbara Hodges, Kent Ross, Debbie Thomas, Duncan MacQuarrie, Rob MacGregor, Stuart Johnston, John Pickett, Norbert Owart, Kathy Temple, Jeff Jones, Dave Atlas, George Hugo, Pat Carlson, David Anderson and many others.

I appreciate conversations with John Morelock, Emmaline Hoffmeister, James Huckabay and Lisa Norris and their good advice in helping me find a way to publish this book.

I thank *UltraRunning*, the flagship publication for the sport, for permission to use, with modification, the first chapter of this book, which originally appeared in that magazine.

My home town (Ellensburg, Washington) newspaper, the *Daily Record*, has published many of these stories. I thank them for doing so, and for permission to use modified versions in this book.

ABOUT THE AUTHOR

David Lygre was peacefully teaching chemistry at Central Washington University, enjoying time with his young family, when he started running thirty-five years ago to lose weight. Then things got out of hand: 100-mile trail runs; chasing national age group records; and, later in life, discovering the joys of bicycling long distances, especially with friends.

His day job lasted 38 years, during which he was honored as Distinguished University Professor for Teaching, Scholar of the Year, and inducted into the Athletics Hall of Fame.

This is his fourth book. Two were chemistry textbooks, but don't hold that against him. His other book, *Life Manipulation*, was an Alternate Selection by the Book-of-the-Month Club.

He is an empty-nester and lives with his wife, Laurae, in Ellensburg, Washington.

Made in the USA
San Bernardino, CA
20 August 2014